ENOUGHNESS

*the simple truth
to embracing
YOU.*

ALISON ROBERTSON

She Creates
Publishing

19818 Hatton St., Winnetka, CA 91306

ISBN: 978-0-578-47145-7 (print)

Ordering Information:
Special discounts are available on quantity purchases by corporations, associations, and others. For details, contact She Creates Publishing.

To my Modern Family.

And to my children,
Corey, Ava & Olivia, who made it a reality.

Acknowledgments

This book wouldn't be possible without the patience, the talents and the gifts of Jessica Abrams, she took my thoughts, my fears and hopes and helped this venture become a reality. She helped me fill the white space.

To my right hand, Melissa Pressman, for her unwavering belief in all things me. May everyone have a champion like Melissa, no words can encompass my gratitude for her. Everything in my world spins in the right direction because she makes sure of it.

Robert Boris for always believing in me, Blake McIver for always seeing me correctly, Kevin E West for never letting up, Adam Salandra for rescuing me with your talent, Wendy Miller for your truth bombs.

For Kathy McCarthy, for giving me the greatest gift.

To my girl squad Robin Stewart, Laurie Records, Sarah Cook, Emily Kerns, Kristen Gifford Mansour, and Amber Ledush.

For the constant support from Natalie & Remy Wallace, Benjie Pressman, Dr. Joan Browner, Mark Teschner, Steven Tyler O'Conner, Michael Lazarovitch, Kessley McCormick, Connie & George Eckmann, and Spencer Strong Smith for being a reflection of me.

Thank you to Anna Halberg for planting the seed to write a book and then SAG Conservatory for allowing me to speak and letting that seed grow...

Much gratitude to Book Launchers for your guidance and unbelievable patience. To GraceWright Productions for jumping in and helping bring the audiobook to life.

To all my clients who have come through my door, who put their trust in me and who, in turn I have learned the most from, I thank you.

I am so grateful for being a Jersey girl. I believe most of my moxie comes from growing up in the Garden State with the family I was blessed with. I can't thank my parents, Ed and Marie, enough for giving me the life that they have. I am blessed to be theirs. I am glad they only made one. Deep down I like to be special and they made sure of that my whole life and still continue to, to this day, making me feel that way. I love you both very much… I hope you are proud

Finally

Thank you Gram… I am who I am because of you.

I Believe to be complete you have to have Enoughness. Enoughness can include but is not limited to the following:

Satisfied

Full

Whole

Complete

Bigger

Grateful

Sufficient

Adequate

Ample

Satisfactory

Expansive

Wide

Great

Comprehensive

Solid

Satiated

Entire

Encompassing

Detail

Immersed

Entire

Successful

Engaged

Obsessed

Robust

Happiness

Delight

Enjoyment

Comfort

Fulfillment

Joy

Bliss

Ecstasy

Rapture

Contentment

Peace

Sound

Calm

Quiet

Stillness

Serenity

Authentic

Healthy

Direct

Source

Wise

Empowered

Stress Free

Confident

Precious

Jubilation

Super Human

Equalize

Poise

Stabilize

Genuine

Cheer

Humor

Laughter

Wonder

Indulgence

Kindness

Believer

Intentional

Author's Note

How to Let This Book Work for You

In order for this book to really work for you, I'm going to ask you to have some faith, a little in me and a lot in you. I know it's hard to trust when we don't see an immediate transformation, especially in our fast-paced world. But just as the caterpillar will someday transform into the butterfly so will you; if you give yourself the time and the space to allow the transformation to happen. The caterpillar isn't running around every day freaking out that something hasn't happened yet. It just is and allows nature to take its course. That's what I'm asking of you here: To believe you can, without evidence that it will happen. Think of this book as your Mother Nature, giving you permission to believe in your infinite potential and possibility.

Remember what it was like as child when we first learned about the wonders around us? Everything felt just a little magical and amazing. The difference now is: You're not a child. You've had a multitude of life experiences. These experiences have formed the way you look at the world and your place in it. You now know, logically, what is happening in the world around you.

Somewhere deep within us all is an innocent child who wants to believe. And just as believing is the first step in creating; wanting to believe makes believing easier. It allows the mental portal to open and the mind to see things differently. So, let go of your notions of impossibility and hardship. Lose the caveats—those obstacles we create in our minds that prevent us from doing something even before we try. Lean into a new way of thinking that believes in miracles.

I don't just want you to survive in this world; I want you to thrive, to soar, and to reach your highest potential.

 *"A jack of all trades is a master of none, but often times better than a master of one."*

What happens when you hear, "You're a Jack of all Trades"? Does it make you feel incomplete? Does it make you feel like you've still got a lot of work to do to find success? Our culture has flipped this saying on its head. This was meant as a compliment. Being a Jack of All Trades is not a bad thing. It means you are able to adapt and pick up things quickly. I think it's important to get this out of the way, right up front. Because of the work you will be doing in this book, you are going to find there are so many facets to you, and that's okay. We get to embrace them all. We get to be complete. We don't have to be a master of one to have a successful and fulfilling life.

So the next time someone calls you a Jack of all Trades, take it as the compliment it was originally meant to be.

Contents

Introduction

Trust that everything happens for a reason,
even when you're not wise enough to see it.

~ OPRAH

You want a bigger life. If you could draw it, it would move off the page. If you could sing it, it would be an aria from Carmen with the shutters flying open, or a full-on air guitar version of Bon Jovi's "Living on a Prayer." If you could wear it, it would be a diamond-encrusted Liberace suit, or a fairy dress that for some reason we stopped wearing when we were six. Deep down you yearn for it the way you ache for that perfect bite of cheesecake at one in the morning. You know it's your right, even if your family, friends, and coworkers will do everything in their power to minimize it. You want the kind of life that, when your head hits the pillow, after you've washed, toned, brushed, and flossed, you know you gave everything, and then some. And I'm not talking about the kind of giving that leaves you feeling empty and disconnected from yourself; I'm talking about the kind of giving that makes you feel connected—not just to others but to yourself in the truest form of oneness that reminds you why you were put on this planet.

I'm talking about living your authentic life, and I'm talking about living it fully.

What does that mean, exactly? These days it seems like every checkout counter at Whole Foods offers magazines advertising how you can get in touch with your authenticity. Retreats providing everything from sweat lodges to yoga (to yoga in sweat lodges) that promise transformations over the course of a (very hot) weekend. I'm by no means discounting any of these methods—I've even done a few myself (not yoga, though; yoga and I have never been on great terms); I'm just letting you know that I'm well aware of how bombarded we are with that kind of information. How it might all start to sound the same—like white noise.

Living an authentic life means being true to who you are and what you want. It doesn't mean that every waking minute will be blissful—in fact, sometimes quite the opposite. It simply means that our thoughts, actions, and goals are in alignment with who we feel we are and what we want; despite what the world may insist is best for us. Other people will support the *should*—your mother, sister, boss, friend. It's my job and yours to support the *want*.

I have always been someone who loves helping others. I have found that works best when I listen closely for that voice in others that may just be a whisper. It's a voice that says *please see the artist I am.* It begs, *please hear that I'm smarter than I may come off.* It's my gift to be able to validate that voice and, like a conductor with an orchestra of one, amplify it and turn it into a shout. That's what I'd like to do for you with this book.

ENOUGHNESS
The Simple Truth of Embracing You

"When your light is on and you are your authentic self, you will be seen."

~ ALISON ROBERTSON

I'm just going to say up front: I don't have rules. There are many ways to live a life, and there are many ways to read this book. As a certified solution-focused coach, I created my own firm in 2010. Once I started working one-on-one with people, I realized how much "rules" got in the way. So many people are following rules they have created for themselves that are in no way benefitting them. I have said many times to those who walk through my door, "If you're following a rule book, may I see it so I know how to help you best." They usually look at me like I'm crazy. They have no idea how much those "rules" are influencing their life. This is why it is so important to me that my book does not create any rules but instead helps guide you towards what you really want.

Each chapter can be viewed as a step, with each step asking you to challenge a habit or a way of thinking that may no longer serve you as you move toward the life you want. Or each chapter can stand on its own. In other words, you can look at the chapters like a prix fixe menu at a three-star Michelin restaurant, where you wouldn't dream of skipping the salad to get to the dessert, or you can treat them like a buffet in Vegas and put the apple pie on your plate right next to the mashed potatoes. It's up to you. My only suggestion is that you be honest with yourself about:

- Who you are
- Where you are now
- What you *want* deep down
- What you *need* day-to-day

That leads me to another subject. I'm bringing this up early so you're in the right frame of mind. H.A.L.T. – Hungry, Angry, Lonely, Tired. We know the state: It creeps up when we've been sitting in traffic having skipped lunch after the baby kept us up all night. Throw in a bad conversation with the credit card company and it's not pretty. The point is, when we're in that state, it's not a good time to ask yourself the tough life questions. It's probably not a good time to ask the easy life questions. It's not a good time to really do much of anything besides eat and watch a few episodes of a favorite show. So, if you find yourself in a state of HALT, please do. This book will still be here when you come back. This is not actually *my* subject, I'll get into my philosophy and sources as we go on, but I want to take a moment to acknowledge that great philosophies can come from anywhere. This one happens to be a major one used in every 12-step program and I find it to be a useful life tool, regardless of your situation.

My tools will appear throughout. Think of them as little elves helping you assemble that piece of Ikea furniture. One hands you a screwdriver while the other digests those confounding instructions. Notice they're not building the piece of furniture with the funny name *for* you. They're empowering you to do it yourself and maybe even go back and do it again, minus the name calling of the little smiley man in the instructions. By picking up this book you're generating a call-to-action to build a new life, and these are the tools you'll need.

And one more thing: Reward yourself. Often and heartily. Transformation comes when we acknowledge the gains we've made, even if it's simply reading a chapter and completing an exercise. The world may not understand what a big step it was for you to make that happen but you do and that's all that matters. Enjoy it. Let it wash over you. Now go get a massage.

*What screws us up
most in life
is the picture of how
it was supposed to be.*

- UNKNOWN

1

Whose Rule Book is it Anyway?

Everyone who has ever opened up a copy of PEOPLE Magazine, or read a biography of Henry Ford, or had a mother, has developed an idea of how life is supposed to turn out. Our culture consumes rags-to-riches stories the way it consumes microwave popcorn—hungrily and fastly. And, to continue with the metaphor, just like microwave popcorn, we tend to lose sight of the process involved with going from inedible kernel to a springy, salty snack.

There's nothing wrong with letting these stories inspire and motivate us. But when that picture in our head turns into the voice of Ray's belittling mother on Everybody Loves Raymond, constantly reminding us that because we didn't turn into the son she wanted, we don't deserve to take up space on the couch – well, that's a sign we may have some reprogramming to do.

Blowing up the picture means different things to different people. That's because everyone has a different snapshot in their head that affects them in a unique way. Some are good, some are not so good. All are worth examining. Sometimes a blowtorch is required. Other times it may simply mean revisiting and reexamining old perceptions. All of these are processes. And if they're going to change your life for the better, they're going to take longer than that bag of microwave popcorn.

Whatever the process or means you need to "blow up your picture," embrace it. Know that there is no right or wrong way, just as long as you are able to move forward. As soon as you blow up the old picture, then you get to create the new picture to replace it.

Sometimes Life Blows Up the Picture for You

My father is a living, breathing example of the American dream. He grew up in a small town in New Jersey, doing what a lot of small town American boys do: He played football. He was the quarterback and had been offered scholarships to two state schools. He may not have been pro material but he was going to use the experience he got from playing football and the opportunities that were offered to him to become a high school football coach. Then fate intervened on October 28, 1961. During a heated game. He went down in a head-on tackle. His neck was broken.

Miraculously, he survived. He did more than survive: He stood up and walked again. So, what does an 18 year old do when his dreams and scholarships have just gone up in smoke? Did I mention he didn't have the funds for college? Now, more than ever, he was determined to get his degree, even if he had to pay for it on his own. Unfortunately, when he got to the school, he was told by a guidance counselor he would not be able to pursue the career he wanted. After his accident the school would not allow it, there was too much physical activity required of him and too much risk. Here's where the story really begins, this counselor gave my dad advice that day that not only changed the course of his life but also, later, set up my path as well. He let him know that he was the luckiest man on the planet and having survived what he did, he should be grateful and try to figure out why he was left on this planet, because there was a reason. My dad has always had an entrepreneurial spirit, even as a young boy and knew he would do well in the business world. He decided he would set his sights on business management.

No doubt there are people who have achieved their goals and reached the milestones they set out to accomplish. What often sets these people apart is an awareness of their gifts versus their passion—which we'll get to in Chapter 5. If you are one of these lucky people, feel free to skip ahead. Or you can read on, because in the work I do I've come to realize that everyone has some kind of nagging "mother" in their head, telling them they've failed because they didn't become an astronaut, or a star soprano, or a blissfully married person with a big family…living in a big house…with a big staircase… on which you frequently pose for pictures (how many of us felt like hell growing up because that Brady Bunch was so damned happy?).

Where do these pictures come from? The truth is, they're like termites—they come from anywhere and everywhere, but you don't really see them until you're on the brink of blowing up the house. They are our lost dreams. Our perceived failures. Our lingering resentments. They're the time our brother borrowed the car and made us late for that college admissions interview. We still wonder how our life would have been different had we gotten there on time. They're the stories we've been carrying with us our entire lives.

My dad could have easily gone down the "woe is me" path; he had been physically taken off course in the most dramatic way. But instead, he made the choice to make his life bigger. He started to embrace his entrepreneurial spirit.

He got into sales, working for a company with the decidedly unglamorous name of U.S. Pipe. Because he was being true to whom he was he made a good impression on his boss. Very soon he and this same boss went into a partnership. They were reps for a piece of machinery called a water blaster; it had the ability to clean the inside of a nuclear reactor. From there they started doing contracts with different energy companies. At one point, they were awarded a contract that felt a little out of their comfort zone. They tried to pass it off to a major energy company who was not interested, so my dad, being who he is, started a company with his partner. Within a decade, he and his partner had built a multimillion-dollar company, helming a firm of 150 employees. Eventually, it was bought by the same Fortune 500 company who turned down the initial contract.

Sometimes, in the moment, we may not realize why things are happening. That night in October, my dad had his life path removed, but what if we could look at it another way. What if we saw the blowing up of the picture as a chance for our true path to emerge?

"When you really pay attention, everything is your teacher."

~ EZRA BAYDA

By "blow up", I don't mean make bigger, I mean set fire to it and watch it shrivel into a hundred charred little pieces. I mean fill a large garbage bag with all the ideas of what you thought life would be and remove it from your house permanently. Important to note, though: Blowing up the picture doesn't mean we throw the past away. If anything, we need to think of the past as teaching a lesson, which provided the skills, wisdom and understanding that we have today. No, we're not negating our past at all. We're letting go of our idea of our past and how it informs our present. We're surrendering a narrative that often has us casting ourselves in the role of the underdog, the victim, the one who never quite gets it right. It's a constant process. I'm still doing it. Drive by my house at any hour and you may see smoke coming out of the windows.

A vision is not just a picture of what could be; it is an appeal to our better selves, a call to become something more.

~ ROSABETH MOSS KANTER

I am very fortunate to have grown up with a father whose luck and keen business instincts took him on this journey. As his daughter, I certainly enjoyed the benefits of his success and the life he had built for my mother and me. But the ease with which success came to him, and in which we lived our lives, did not make for ease when it came to following my own path, if that makes any sense. My parents knew struggle, and if you're a parent or anyone who has taken care of someone, you will understand the logic that followed. My parents' love for me was so great, the last thing they wanted for me was to go through any kind of struggle or hardship. They put in the work so I wouldn't have to. Things were given to me before I could even formulate a question and ask for them. My parents' nurturing skills were so well refined that they provided for me before I even knew what I needed or even wanted. Do you know how empowering it is to ask for something? Just hearing yourself say what you want solidifies the desire; then when a parent—or anyone—tells us "no", we fortify ourselves by oftentimes pushing for it anyway. That's when we realize how much we really want something and how to get it, come hell or high water. Without intending to—as a matter of fact, with nothing but pure, unadulterated love—my parents managed to disempower me.

In following my dream to become an actor, (which is a profession where "struggle" is built into the job description) I lacked any awareness of what this path would require of me. I somehow thought my career would simply be an extension of my life. How wrong I was. My father's picture of his future got blown up that evening on the football field. I had two pictures to blow up: One that said my life would be as pothole-free as my parents set it up to be. The other said that I didn't need to cultivate the tools to navigate the blocks and hurdles that did arise. That someone would always "take care of it" for me—that someone would always take care of *me*. Let me be clear, I never threw myself a "my parents loved me too much, oh poor me" pity party, I simply had some harsh realities to face the moment I left their protective cocoon. The values I learned from them, however, cannot be genetically measured but have been just as vital to me as an inherited external talent: Generosity of mind, means, and meatballs. Always give someone your advice, always give someone what you have, and always give someone a meal.

The Day My Picture Blew Up

Now on my own, I quickly realized I couldn't keep up the New York pace or more accurately the New York cost of living. I went to do Summer Stock in Charlotte, NC. I found a little TV enclave there where I could be a big fish in a small pond and easily afford the rent. I was an actor there, and it was empowering. During Summer Stock, I booked a commercial. In the commercial I had a six-year-old son. The morning of the shoot the six year old came up to me and said, "Do you want to play hangman?" I said, "NO!" After his third request I finally conceded to play one round only. He laid down a 14-letter word. I was irate. I thought to myself, "What the hell happened to cat?" The word was *paleontologist.* This was not your ordinary kid actor. As I played that game of hangman, which I lost by the way, an incredible thing happened. I felt the skills instilled in me by my parents flood over me. I had no idea they had been lying dormant, waiting for the moment I was needed.

Unfortunately, it wasn't flawlessly spelled out to me like Moses and the burning bush. Instead I had three thoughts: 1) I'm going to know this little boy forever, 2) He's going to make a million dollars, 3) I'm going to need therapy. Two out of these three have happened.

Here's why I'm telling you this story: This six-year-old boy named Corey needed me. I could've ignored it completely, left the set that day and gone on with my life. But remember those things I inherited from my parents? They now had an intense purpose. I had advice, means, and quite a few great meals to give to this child. The specifics of how Corey ended up part of my family a few years later and we raised him up through college are not vital to the point here. The point is I blew up the picture I had of my future, in the biggest way possible. Did I raise some eyebrows? Certainly. Did I make some people uncomfortable throughout the process? Absolutely. But if I hadn't answered the call that day and been afraid of stepping into a territory that I barely knew I had the tools for, my life would have never been the journey of enrichment, empowerment and nurture that it has been with Corey.

He forced me to shed the idea I had of myself. He forced me to move past my own perceived limitations. He forced me to grow up—or rather, I forced myself to grow up when I listened to that little voice inside, which called me to be bigger than I could even imagine. There wasn't room for my new self in my old plan, so yes, I had to blow up my picture and rebuild again with my new self in mind. As I've said before, there are many ways our pictures can be blown up. My dad's happened in a very physical way. But sometimes, like with me, it's not as dramatic. It can be as simple as a ___ coming into your life. Whatever it is, just remember, *things happen for us not to us.*

Things Happen for Us, Not to Us

Before we can set fire to the snapshot of life (as it was supposed to happen, *dammit),* we need to do a little revisionist history where our life events are concerned. First of all, I have news for you: The past is over and there's no changing it. That's a hard pill to swallow because most people, myself included from time to time, love to dwell in the past. We go back to the time we turned down the job, fell for the wrong person or said the wrong thing to the wrong boss. We subconsciously think that the more we dwell, the more we'll figure out "where we went wrong".

I have two words for you: *Groundhog Day.* Trying to figure out where we went wrong often just keeps us in the same pattern of wrong-ness, if you can call it that. It keeps us stuck between two extremes: That we are powerless victims, or we are complete screwups who ran our lives amok. I have news for you: neither one of these mindsets helps us to move forward.

The energy it takes to hang onto the past is holding you back from a new life.

~ MARY MANIN MORRISSEY

What if we tweaked our perception? What if we chose to look at things that seemed to have happened *to* us and decided that, in fact, they happened *for* us? What if we viewed setbacks/bad luck/disappointments—whatever they've been branded with that mental rubber stamp—as gifts that led us down a path that was ultimately more right for us than the one we were initially dead set on following?

The Prison of "Should"

It doesn't take more than 30 seconds for anyone to identify what they "should" be doing in their lives. Whether this "should" stems from an internal expectation or a perceived external judgment is irrelevant. The point is that this concept of "should" is as crippling as the four walls of a prison cell. The sooner we can free ourselves from our own prison of "should" and our idea—*which is wholly of our own* making—of the way things are supposed to be, the sooner we can embrace ourselves in our exquisite fullness and live the life we want.

I'll go into more detail in Chapter 5, but my own personal prison of "should" took its hold in my acting career. I was so set on working in entertainment that I became completely petrified that if I did anything else, at any time, I was no longer an actor. I "should" only focus on this one career path if I were to succeed. Had I given into the "should" and ignored all my other talents and skills, I can't imagine how one-dimensional my life would have been. And quite frankly, you wouldn't be reading this book right now.

And for the record, I didn't lose a career path, I became bigger. And damn if it didn't also make me a better actor and more successful in the process.

I challenge you to say "yes". And I'm sure you'll find various examples of gains you've made in life that were a direct result of things not working out as you had planned. You hear stories about people diagnosed with cancer who suddenly get a new lease on life. Would they have decided to volunteer with orphans in Vietnam or gone to culinary school if they hadn't been diagnosed with a potentially life-threatening illness? We'll never know. You don't need a traumatic event to spur radical change. You just need some clarity. And a pack of matches.

Letting Go and Experiencing Gratitude

It's not always easy to reframe an entrenched idea, especially if that idea has managed to seep into our psyches and color our sense of self. Compassion and gratitude are the only way out of these entrenched ideas and negative cycles of thought. Start by simply being grateful for what you have done. Finished paying off your car? Hallelujah! Learned how to cook your own meals and stay healthy? Awesome! Created your own business? Woohoo! When it comes to feeling and expressing gratitude, it's important to remember that *there's no size requirement.* If anything, being grateful and proud for the small things creates a better internal breeding ground for the big ones. Feeling good brings good things in.

"If you know your WHY, you can find your dream."

~ ALISON ROBERTSON

2

Dancing Around
Your Dream

I Have a Dream

The word "dream" when used to describe something envisioned during waking hours is, by and large, an American concept. From the ideas laid down by the founding fathers in the Declaration of Independence to Martin Luther King Jr.'s iconic speech, we are a culture that sprang forth around a vision of a better life for our loved ones and ourselves. We may not have known exactly what that dream looked like but we took a leap of faith into the great unknown in order to make it manifest.

We may use the word "dream" a lot but we Americans are not the only people who are ready to risk everything to make our dreams reality. The fact is, having a vision of what you want for your life is part of the human condition. It is a sign of a higher consciousness. A shelter dog may wish for a home but we have yet to hear that he or she made a vision board showing us just what that home looks like.

And maybe you haven't either. Maybe you're not quite sure what your dream looks like, or that you even have one. Maybe you didn't even know you needed a WHY to find your dream.

A dream can be a banana split or a single scoop of Italian gelato. It can encompass various facets of your world, or be the one thing that's missing from a near-perfect life. You can even be living it right now.

It's not easy to stake our claim on a dream. It feels risky. Why? Because it is. Most people don't follow their dreams. They give up on them in favor of an easier path. There's nothing wrong with that but that's not why you're reading this book. Sometimes, even if we think we're on the path, we're not—or rather, we're dancing around the path because it's safer. We're playing tricks on ourselves to avoid the real work. The aspiring entrepreneur who's working in someone else's startup as opposed to getting his or her own business off the ground and becoming financially independent. The musician who writes music for commercials and yet deep down wants to write her own stuff. That fantastic aunt or uncle who puts off having a family of his or her own, even though it's a deep-seated want.

We have to make money and oftentimes the best and most rewarding way to do it is in our chosen field. But it's important to be mindful of whether we're gaining valuable knowledge and experience to apply to our own endeavors, or if it enables us to tell ourselves we're getting closer to our dream when we're really not.

Dare to Dream

For some of us, life is pretty good right now—good job, kids doing okay—and the last thing you want is to rock the boat and ask for something bigger and scarier than the comforts in front of you. Or you've always wanted to do something but just don't know how to say, "I want to do this", with no apologies. Maybe you just know there's another way to live, even if you don't know exactly how it looks. Perhaps you're like Wayne—who, as a successful salesman with the ability to generate a great income, needed major prodding from me before he was finally able to admit he had a dream. What he really wanted was a house, a loving wife and kids—and not in that order. He wanted—drumroll please—*a home.* Now his work has focus. *He* has focus. He now has a strong *WHY.* Before he was able to openly acknowledge his dream, he felt like that poor hamster, stuck on that damned wheel, unsatisfied and unfocused.

It's not easy to break down the idea of a dream, but I would say if you're unsure about your dreams, consider this:

What does your heart say? You don't have to be perfect and know your exact path—the truth is, most of us don't—but what speaks to you in a way nothing else does? What connects you to something deep inside you that makes you feel alive? Try looking for signs in events from the past, how you're living in the present and what you envision for your future. For example:

- What kinds of activities did you find yourself doing a lot as a child *that you truly enjoyed?* Did you put on plays in the backyard? Play an instrument—one that *you* wanted to play, as opposed to one a parent pushed you to play?

- Do you have a hobby, a cause, or a course of study that you're involved with that you enjoy so much you lose track of time while you're doing it? Something that makes you feel connected to who you are on a very basic level?

- When you think of your ideal future—keyword is "ideal", so now's not the time to be practical—

what do you see yourself doing/having/being?

See if that doesn't get the wheels turning.

There Is a Difference Between a Dream and an Escape Plan

Be mindful when you have the urge to flee. Whether that's part of your dream or a way of avoiding it, there's something to be said for the famous quote from Voltaire's Candide, "We must cultivate our garden." Let's start where we are now and see what we can grow from it.

A dream is, well, that thing you've always wanted, that no matter how much you talk yourself out of, when you hear someone else is doing it, you start to feel hot all over and maybe a little nauseous. You're not sure what happened because, well, you thought you'd shoved that idea aside in favor of a more practical plan. But apparently not. So you chastise yourself, get back into your life and the pattern repeats. How many times does the pattern have to repeat before you get the message?

An escape plan is just the opposite: It's a way for you to avoid life, which includes your dreams. It's the tropical island that comes to mind five minutes after you've been called into the boss' office and offered a hefty raise. It's an easy out, a way to avoid dealing with the larger questions life asks of us. There's nothing wrong with vacations or time away from the routine, but an escape plan is more than a vacation. It's a sharp left turn off the road of life onto a new road. This road may be freshly paved and lined with flowers, but it just keeps going with no endpoint. And there's not a gas station in sight.

One way to tell if you're daring to dream or seeking an escape is to ask yourself if the following equation applies to you:

If I do X, then I will feel Y.

Are you desperate to relieve a momentary feeling or are you seeking a long-range goal? Are you hoping for a quick fix or are you focusing on the bigger picture?

My Escape Plan

Immediately after I gave birth to my younger daughter Olivia, I had the urge to go to New Orleans and help the victims of Hurricane Katrina. When I say I had the urge to go, I don't mean that I was thinking about leaving in a few months' time. No—I was this close to buying a plane ticket before a couple of wise souls in the form of my kid's dad and my mother stepped in and yanked the credit card from my hand. Mind you, I'm all in favor of being of service but when you've got a child that's just a few months old—well, that may not be the best time to indulge in those selfless tendencies.

I had this burning urge because I wanted to flee. I wanted to run from my crying baby and the task in front of me. That the victims of Katrina were almost as helpless as my baby didn't cross my mind; I just wanted to get on a plane, hand out food and blankets, be thanked for them, and forget about what I had just taken on. I hadn't yet accepted the gifts in front of me and was still allowing "should" to color who I thought I was and what I needed to do to be a great mom.

I was allowing fear to drive my decisions. But how do we get out of that fear, how do we let the escape plan go? The antidote to breaking out of the fear is to ground yourself back in your WHY; this is why the WHY is so important.

There is nothing like a dream to create the future.

~ VICTOR HUGO

A dream is a life that we know deep down is ours to live. It's an idea that utilizes our highest self and gives us our WHY, the driving force that gets us there. It's a desire that comes from the depths of your soul, and ideally the pursuit of it should feed your soul as much as the achieving of it. It speaks to your uniqueness and the fact that there is only one of you in this entire world.

Your Dreams in a Trust

Are you like my friend, Jennifer, who could no longer ignore her dream and chose to become an actor in her forties?

Trust me, she had plenty of outside sources telling her this was impossible. Sure, certain endeavors may not get easier as we get older, and starting them may require more hard work than others, but if your dream was earmarked for you, why can't it be waiting for you to claim it? The late actor, Kathryn Joosten, of *West Wing* and *Desperate Housewives* fame didn't start acting until she was in her forties. Grandma Moses began a painting career in her seventies. Colonel Sanders started his famous chicken franchise in his sixties. Christian Dior founded the House of Dior at 41. Jennifer's WHY was so strong she was able to tune out the outside noise of "it's too late" and her mother's desire for her to have a "stable" job. She went for it and I can tell you, she couldn't be happier.

You are never too old to set another goal or to dream a new dream.

~ C.S. LEWIS

EXERCISE

Sit where you're comfortable and there are no grating noises setting your teeth on edge. If you're hungry, go eat. If you need to send that email, go do it.

❧

When you're ready, let's go on a little ride. What if a genie in a pair of colorful harem pants were to materialize out of that bottle of Pinot Noir you were drinking? Stay with me here. And what if he told you that he would grant you one wish, and with that wish you could have the life you wanted? What would it look like? What would you eat for breakfast? What kind of coffee would you drink and how would it be made? How much sunlight would stream into your kitchen?

What about work? What would you do? Would you work at home in a cozy, book-lined office or go into a high-rise where your 50 employees would be waiting for you? What kind of work would it be? Maybe it doesn't even feel like work— maybe it sounds like so much fun you can't even imagine calling it "work." And yet you get paid lots of money to do it—and you're happy.

For some of us, the dream consists of a collection of images that we can almost touch, smell, and feel: Cotton sheets fresh from the dryer. A house with an ocean view. For others, it's experiential: Starting their own business. Writing a novel. Going into politics. Or saving the world.

～◯～

Do this for three days. See where it takes you. I have a sneaky suspicion you will find your WHY.

To be yourself in a world that is constantly trying to make you something else is the greatest accomplishment.

~ RALPH WALDO EMERSON

3

How Does the World
See You?

Who Am I?

It's hard to think of three words that have caused as much anxiety or generated as much interest as these three have. They're the engines behind industries that range from personal development (guilty as charged), to psychology, to advertising, to cosmetics and I've probably missed a few. It's easy to write this phenomenon off as being part of a collective obsession with personality and self, but I would posit that there's a deeper motive behind our love of the Buzz Feed quiz. We need to know who we are deep down, to understand the workings of our psyches and our temperaments, to comprehend our motives and reactions. And, thanks to the work of doctors Freud and Jung—the Lewis and Clark of the inward journey—we have the ability to do it.

Who am I? Chances are if you're reading this book you've probably asked that question more than once. Whether you've wondered *what kind of screen siren are you?* Or delved into psychoanalysis, there are many reasons why you might want to fulfill Socrates' command to "know thyself". Why? Because understanding our habits and patterns, our triggers and tendencies, is the first step in evolving. Understanding the "why" in our behavior allows us to modify it. There are many ways to solve the mystery of you. Some are fun and have the amazing effect of making us feel less alone. A good biography can do that with the added bonus of inspiring us: *If Katherine Hepburn was like that, maybe there's hope for me.* Other mysteries require more commitment and emotional heavy lifting.

We're not going to delve into your family dynamics here, or determine what type you are on the Myers-Briggs scale. I am neither a psychologist nor a Jungian analyst, although I support both and whatever else you may need to dive into those murkier waters. I've been helped immensely by therapy myself. What I am is a solution-focused coach, which means I'm very skilled at working with the information in front of me to move you from where you are now to where you want to be.

By taking a deeper look at ourselves, we get to see certain parts of our personality for what they are: Habits that can be broken. Patterns that can be retrained. Also, those quizzes are just kind of fun. I'm Rita Hayworth, by the way.

Limiting Self Beliefs

In her now world-famous quote, spiritual teacher Marianne Williamson (http://marianne.com) (posits) that, "Our deepest fear is not that we are inadequate. Our deepest fear is that we are powerful beyond measure. It is not our darkness but our light that frightens us." She goes on to say, "We ask ourselves, who am I to be brilliant, gorgeous, talented, fabulous? Actually, who are you not to be? You are a child of God. Your playing small does not serve the world."

Many of us had parents that sought to lower our expectations about life. They may have done it unknowingly, simply to prevent disappointment, or they carried with them certain resentment about their own truncated dreams. Even the most enlightened parents can't help but bring their own baggage into the child-rearing mix, and that includes their insecurities and sense of self-doubt and whatever baggage *their* parents bequeathed them. It's almost unavoidable. Growing up, you may have heard, "You're not good with numbers", because of your father's insecurities with math. Or maybe your mother's dislike of her looks made her less than complimentary towards yours. The point is, we become conditioned to see ourselves in a certain way based on what we heard as children. But here's what's miraculous: *We don't have to take it on.* We can make an active choice to dismantle that legacy and ask for more. And not just ask, *be* more. Who are we *not* to be brilliant, gorgeous, talented, and fabulous indeed?

How do we do that? We start by noticing thought patterns. We pay close attention to those moments when we speak words to ourselves like "always" and "never". If you lock your keys in the car, do you suddenly recall every time, going back to when you were five, that you exhibited a certain absentmindedness? Don't get me wrong—all patterns and habits should be open to review and evaluation; if you are consistently distracted, that's something worth noting and possibly modifying. But beating yourself up with messages like, "Why am I always such a dunce?" or "I'm so stupid" keeps us locked in a limited view of ourselves that doesn't move us forward. Don Miguel Ruiz (http://www.miguelruiz. com), in his book, *The Four Agreements,* refers to the sum total of these messages as *the book of law* that rules our mind. The process of maintaining this set of "agreements", as he calls them, robs us of our personal power and keeps us in a state of suffering.

My dear friend, Rebecca, always heard, "You're so funny," as throwaway words. In her mind, the subtext of that was always, "You're not to be taken seriously." It wasn't until we started having long chats over glasses of wine together and *I* started telling her that in earnest that she began to embrace her humor in every aspect of her life. Rebecca *is* funny. That's who she is. It's not the only thing she is but it's the tip of the iceberg of a personality that sees the irony in life, that mitigates darkness by making a joke and strives to connect to people.

Let's start with the words people have used to describe you, even if, like Rebecca, you've always considered them throwaway comments. "You're so sweet," when said often enough has real meaning. It indicates an open heart, a generous spirit, and a trusting personality that sees the good in people. "You're so smart," also carries more weight than we often give it. My friend, Roger, heard those words all his life but wrote them off. He had never been a particularly good student and in his head, "You're so smart," was always followed by, "Why can't you do better?" But once I got him to look past whatever expectations he did or didn't live up to, he began to realize that in fact he was capable of extremely sophisticated thinking—*on his terms*. He was smart, yes— but he really excelled in subjects that interested him. And when they did, his thoughts and theories on those matters were brilliant.

Pay attention to what you've heard and what you hear. Even, "You're awesome," is something to take in. It means, at least for that moment, you have inspired awe in someone. Be careful about dismissing comments and adjectives because your brain has turned them into veiled insults. That's unfortunately what we humans do. Often the more sophisticated a mind, the more likely it is to twist a positive into a negative. There is a popular saying that goes, "If it's hysterical, it's historical," meaning that past experience can muddy our thinking, turning truth into fiction (or fiction into truth).

A great way to connect with who you are on a deep level

is to look at how your friends, your family, your spouse and your coworkers rely on you. Are you the one your girlfriend calls two minutes after she gets off the phone with her now ex-boyfriend, having just learned he does not want to marry her? Or are you the one she calls a week later—after she and her *other* friends have broken the situation down six ways to Sunday (and imbibed those many bottles of wine)—when she needs help moving out from his place? Pay attention to that—these are two different kinds of people.

Do you get called when a friend needs to take a leap of faith or when he needs to play it safe? Do you get asked to bring the main course to the potluck or to just pick up a dessert? And, trust me, the answer does not just have to do with cooking skills. Do friends and family fear your judgment and seek it only when they're ready to hear it? Or do they consider you a steady sounding board? Pay attention to these things. Feel free to ask your friends what they rely on you for and why. Be willing to hear the truth.

Unlimit Yourself

Some people can take a lifetime to figure out who they are. For others, they are able to accept who they are much quicker. Take for example my business partner, Melissa. She is the kind of person who knows how to get things done (which is why I can't imagine life without her). Her organizational skills would make Martha Stewart jealous. Melissa has many amazing qualities, but this facet to her personality is one she would be silly not to pay attention to when crafting her life. I love getting to see people have their aha moment, and when she had hers, it turned things around for both of us. She finally saw that part of herself as not just a part but also an actual asset. Once she embraced that it enabled her to enjoy a successful marriage, chase after three boys and run our business.

Show me your friends and I will show you your future.

~ JOHN KUEBLER

Who Are You Drawn To

We all know people who fall in love with temperamental artists. They love the painter who makes art and love with equal parts passion and madness. Maybe that's you—as much as you hate the fact that he's never on time, or that his work always comes first, or he's too broke to take you to a nice restaurant, you're drawn to that sense of abandon, that unfailing commitment to art. Or perhaps you find yourself attracted to more stable personalities—to that man or woman who likes dinner at six and then a couple of hours of television—always the same shows, week after week—before calling it a night and then starting the whole thing over the next day.

Take a hard look at whom you're attracted to, whether it be in friends or romantic partners, because it says a lot about you. Even though the popular line of thinking is "opposites attract", in my work I've found that we're drawn to people— particularly when it comes to romantic relationships—who bring out dormant qualities in ourselves. Note the word **dormant**: It comes from the Latin *dormire*, meaning "to sleep," which means the quality is still present in us, it may just not be active. And we are subconsciously pulled toward the people who will help bring it out. Why? Because deep down we all have an urge to be fulfilled. To make use of all our gifts and faculties. To listen to those voices, however quietly they speak, that tell us we have more to do in this lifetime than our parents, our school, even our own selves have acknowledged. Being attracted to those crazy artists could mean that we have our own artist living inside us who wants to break free of whatever limitations we've placed on ourselves, or that we simply want permission to live life with a little bit of wildness.

 I Am.
Two of the most powerful words;
for what you put after them shapes
your reality.

~ GARY HENSEL

Don't Let One Thing Define You

We live in a country where we define ourselves by what we do to pay rent and feed the cat. Go to France and the first question you're asked is never, "What do you do?" But in the United States, our profession is a determining factor in how we see ourselves and how we connect—be it at a dinner party, a bar or in line at the DMV. Wouldn't it be nice, if instead we were asked, "How do you live?"

There's nothing wrong with being dedicated to a career, but it's important to keep in mind that what we do during the day doesn't define us. As a matter of fact, thinking it does is another way we limit ourselves. I am a doctor. I am a social worker. Does that mean you have an extra limb? No. We're all people. Defining ourselves by what we do can isolate us and hold us back from nurturing our other talents. And sometimes the more time we put into something—going to medical school, becoming a ballet dancer—the more our identity is tied to that endeavor.

Newsflash: Your career is not you. You are you. You will

still be you even if you're a basketball coach who works part time at a restaurant or a hedge fund owner who knits baby booties and sells them online.

I grew up wanting to be an actor. It was the answer I gave whenever an adult posed the oft-asked question, "What do you want to be when you grow up?" It was what I did the minute my parents consented and let me start going to auditions. For many years it was how I supported my family. It's still my great love. But in the last few years I've had to make some adjustments and unearth new gifts in order to make a living. They've brought me here, today, to write this book. I'm still me—the same person I was before I made those shifts—and my passion for acting hasn't diminished. I've just added another moniker to my list: Mother, actor, speaker, coach. Tethering yourself to what you do keeps you small. It keeps you imprisoned in *The Box*. It's also just not good business sense. In my parents' time, people stayed married to one person and worked for one company their entire lives. Now both of those paradigms have shifted. The divorce rate hovers between 42 and 50 percent in the US; and, according to the Bureau of Labor Statistics, the average American will have 10 jobs before the age of 40. Companies no longer offer the same lifelong benefits they did even just one generation ago. We need to be more flexible in our thinking so we can be more flexible in our revenue streams. We need to take care of ourselves instead of handing over the car keys of our life to a corporation or an idea—both of which could drive us over a cliff.

Chances are you have a multitude of talents and passions (and we'll get to gifts versus passion in Chapter 5). So, why actively limit yourself to just one facet of your personality? Why close yourself off to the full spectrum of you? Take those guitar lessons. Volunteer at that animal shelter. What's stopping you?

Comparing Ourselves with Others

There was once a wise old (or young) sage who said, "When you compare, you always lose." It's true. Have you ever heard yourself say, "Even though Susie has a beautiful house, two beautiful children, and a loving, doting husband, my inner life is much richer than hers and therefore I'm at peace with it."? No. When we compare, we always put ourselves at the bottom—even if we *do* have a richer inner life and we know for a fact that Susie is miserable. Don't get me wrong—I don't want Susie to be miserable; I just want you to stop comparing yourself to her or to anyone.

Each of us is uniquely perfect. And "perfect" in this case does not mean the nit-picky, airtight ideal that we impose on ourselves, à la Betty Draper in season one of *Mad Men*. No—in this case I mean the divine perfect, the way we were made before our minds got in the way and messed with nature's work. You see, after we were made, the mold was broken. We each have an individual set of gifts to offer the world and an individualized curriculum to make that happen. We have different parents, backgrounds, stumbling blocks and lessons to learn. Comparing ourselves diminishes those differences. It diminishes us.

Envy is not always a bad thing. Seeing Susie's children can remind us of what we want for ourselves. It can put us in touch with our true desires. But comparing is different. With it comes the presumption that we're all on the exact same path—or worse, that Susie's racing down hers and you're racing down yours, and whoever gets to the beautiful family and house first wins. It also just makes us feel badly about ourselves because we rarely stop with a simple comparison. We begin a narrative that goes back to childhood and brings in every failure, mistake and loss that stops only when sleep comes.

Notice when you find yourself doing it. Head it off at the pass. Cut it off at the knees. It does not serve you.

Pay attention to the messages you tell yourself. Pay extra-special attention to the words, "I can't", that sneak up when a new idea—or an idea you've had forever but have been too afraid to attempt—comes up. It may be so subtle you don't even hear yourself say it—you just dismiss it before your brain can formulate the words. In the case of "I can't", the antidote is to do it. That's right. Listen to Nike and "*Just Do It*". Because the best way to dismantle an old idea is to take an action that will negate it right then and there. And note: I didn't say do it well. I didn't say become an expert at it. I simply said do it, because the message you will then send yourself is that you can. And you did.

I know I threw a lot at you in this chapter, but I promise you, if you sit down with how those around you see you, who you're drawn to and unlimit yourself, you will come to your authentic self. The You that will keep you on your path to your WHY and ultimately your dream.

 Authenticity is the daily practice of letting go of who we think we're supposed to be and embracing who we are.

BRENÉ BROWN

EXERCISE

Think of five people you admire. You don't have to admire every single facet of each of their personalities; think of them as a whole human, flaws and all.

⁓ ⌐

Now use 10 (or more, if they come) words to describe them. Don't think too much, just jot the words down.

⁓ ⌐

Stare at the words. See if they may also describe you just a little bit. If not, can they become a part of your personality? Would doing so possibly help you become a fuller version of the person you want to be?

"Don't lose your
present to your past."

~ ANONYMOUS

4

How'd You Get Here?

The Playlist in Our Head

It's one thing when a parent utters a few harsh words: A couple decades of therapy and you're good to go, right? I'm joking, obviously. But sometimes our own playlists of mistakes and missteps from the past—the ones that, without a doubt, we caused—can be more difficult to sort through. Then it becomes nearly impossible to separate ourselves from an event that happened 20 years ago. It becomes nearly impossible to move forward.

I ran up 50 thousand dollars' worth of credit card debt, so I'm not good with money.

I got fired from Wendy's when I was 16, so I don't have a good work ethic.

My college girlfriend told me I'm not built for relationships so I must not be.

These are examples of phrases that rattle around in our brains and keep us locked in the past. We replay the voice, the situation, and the moment again and again. Or maybe we've simply internalized it so successfully that we don't even remember the source of the idea. We just let it rule our lives.

A Little Background

There are several reasons why humans do this. A negative emotion is tied to our fight-or-flight response. Just as if a tiger were jumping out of a tree a few feet away, this instinct forces us to narrow our focus and respond with a very specific reaction. That's why we get immediately defensive when someone accuses us of something. It's also why we have a difficult time seeing our way past emotions like fear, anger and stress. Negative emotions—including the kind that come from being made to feel like we're not good enough—cause us to focus on the threat, or in this case, the comment. Our rational mind does not stand a chance when faced with this. It's not wired that way. Add a few years into the batter, sprinkle in some more "examples" to support the original claim, and you've rewired your brain and turned a doubt into a reality. As Carl Jung said, "What you resist persists."

At the base of the brain where the head meets the neck, we have what is called the Reticular Activating System, or RAS. Jack Canfield (http://jackcanfield.com), author of the mega-famous *Chicken Soup for the Soul*, among other books, speaks about this. As for me, being a gal who grew up with her feet firmly planted on New Jersey soil and who doesn't always go in for the airy-fairy stuff, this kind of science-based information makes a lot of sense. The RAS is designed to sort data so that we don't become overwhelmed with too much stimuli. You see, at any given moment your senses are relaying thousands of bits of information to your brain. If you had to consciously sort it all, that's all you would do, all day, every day. But aside from sorting out all the extraneous information our senses present every second, it also goes searching for the data it thinks will be helpful to our conscious mind in that moment. It's the reason why we suddenly notice the gazillion fast food restaurants we are driving past when we're hungry, or hear all kinds of weird noises after we've binge-watched *American Horror Story*, and it's midnight and we're alone in the house. The RAS can both help us and hold us back. We'll get to the helping part in a bit; in the meantime, let's explain why the brain can stay focused on the negative unless we set powerful intentions to move our thoughts in another direction. The RAS seeks information that validates your beliefs and helps you see what you want to see and therefore influences our actions. It never shuts down. Notice I didn't say it seeks only positive; it seeks what you tell it. The brain is the most powerful computer we have so what you feed it is very important. As we continue, please keep in mind that the RAS is the powerhouse of motivation and goal setting.

Your Mistakes Don't Define You

You are not your divorce, the job you got fired from, the car you ran off the road. Radical, huh? You are not the relationship where you strayed or the college that didn't accept you. We are all so much more, and the sooner we realize this, the sooner we can move forward. We're also wired so that once we release the ghost from purgatory and let it go permanently, we can begin the process of true transformation.

Unlike guilt, which is the feeling of doing something wrong, shame is the feeling of being something wrong.

~ MARILYN J. SORENSON

The Shame Spiral

Shame is one of the most complex emotions of the human psyche. We know it when we feel it. It can manifest as panic, extreme mortification, even physical illness. It causes us to feel exposed and vulnerable, sometimes in front of another person but most often in front of ourselves. That's the thing about shame: The person we feel exposed to never experiences the same feeling we *think* they're feeling. They may react but chances are they've brushed it off and moved on within minutes. Meanwhile, we're left with a feeling that the word "awful" doesn't even begin to describe. And if we don't catch it, it can send us down a very dark hole, pulling in every incident in which we've felt even remotely like that one. The time we stood on stage in kindergarten and the teacher criticized us. That time our parents caught us kissing our girlfriend in the car. The time you shared your personal essay with the class and they laughed at you.

This is the shame spiral. For some, it leads to a lashing-out completely disproportionate to the incident that inspired the feeling of shame to begin. It works on self-esteem like a wrecking ball, ending relationships and depleting our emotional tank—in a sense, leaving us stranded in the desert with no cell service. In the book, *Facing Shame*, Merle A. Fossum and Marilyn J. Mason (http://www.marilynmason. com) say, "While guilt is a painful feeling of regret and responsibility for one's actions, shame is a feeling about oneself as a person."

John Bradshaw (http://www.johnbradshaw.com) in his book, *Healing the Shame That Binds You*, talks about healthy shame versus toxic shame. Healthy shame is the knowing of limits and the setting of boundaries. Healthy shame includes the permission to make mistakes and ultimately learn from them. It can be the source of both creativity and spirituality. Toxic shame, on the other hand, comes from many sources, including but not limited to being raised in a family with secrets—i.e., addiction, abuse, dysfunction and abandonment. These factors alone can cause toxic shame in a child and if not dealt with as an adult can manifest itself in a host of negative behaviors that just keep us stuck in the shame cycle.

We're diving into deep waters here. In fact, the source of shame can run so deep that I can't pretend to be able to wave a magic wand and make it go away. What I can do is make you aware of how shame can be a trigger, and let you know that when we investigate the early source of our shame and shine a light on it, it can end up being like The Wizard of Oz: A small man sitting behind a big control box. His feet don't even touch the floor and he wears coke-bottle glasses, but he's got all the buttons in front of him, and damn if he isn't going to use each and every one.

The Playbook of "If I Had Only..."

For many of us, one of the offshoots of shame is the habit of meticulously tracing back to one incident that, in our minds, completely sets our lives on a different course. And when I say "different," I mean the *wrong* course, as you've set it up in your mind. We create a story around it: *The time I was too scared to call Susie in high school and ask her to the prom, which explains why I'm not married now. That time I didn't do a good job on that work project and lost the client, and now can't find a decent paying job.* Like all things shame-related, we then pull every related incident in—everything that came after this perceived failure that, in our minds, caused another set of events to happen or not happen. We talked about this in Chapter 1 when we discussed blowing up the picture, but it's important to note that these thought patterns generally begin with shame and, if unchecked, only create more shame.

Remember when I said that the Reticular Activating System could be helpful? Well here's how. It can be used to help set new patterns in place. By taking a concept—an idea of what we want, a goal, an intention for the day— and focusing on it mentally, filling it with whatever positive emotions we may associate with that idea, we create a very powerful intention towards the achievement of that goal. We actually have it in our power to rewire our thought patterns and, ultimately, change our lives.

It's amazing what we carry around as baggage, how we craft narratives about our lives and how that becomes our "story". If you're wondering if you do this, the words "always" and "never" are good indicators. Do you find yourself saying them time and time again to explain yourself—either to others or just in your head? If so, you might want to consider

reframing the narrative or simply tossing it. Another way to shift your outlook is to change the words "I have to" to "I get to". Why is this important? Because "I have to" holds a negative weight. It implies what we are not in control of our day or our lives. "I get to" immediately suggests opportunity and positivity. It's the kind of cognitive reprogramming that not only reconfirms that we're in charge of the course of our lives but also that we are immensely grateful to be in the driver's seat.

Whatever you hold in your mind on a consistent basis is exactly what you will experience in your life.

~ TONY ROBBINS

Do you want some minor missteps—or even not-so minor ones—to dictate your life? Do you want to be like my friend, Sharon who, for the first 30-some-odd years of her life could hear nothing but her crazy mother telling her she wasn't worthy? And every mishap reminded her of that, to the point where she would become stuck in a story/shame spiral that kept her from making use of her multitude of talents and skills? No, you don't.

Don't take your THEN self and put it on your NOW self.

Sometimes it's also easier to forgive others than to forgive ourselves, possibly for the same neurological reason. We expect more from ourselves and hang onto our own mistakes and shortcomings far longer than we do with other people. If someone in our circle does something that annoys or hurts us, chances are we confront them about it. If it *still* doesn't get resolved, we share it with someone else. We tell our other friend/family member/therapist, "I'm annoyed with Allen. He doesn't seem to understand why." And then we work it out a little more with *that* person.

But when we make a mistake or do something that makes us mad at ourselves, we don't necessarily have anyone to talk to. I don't say, "Alison, I'm really upset with you today." And I certainly don't get a response back from myself asking "Why?

What did I do?" I would save myself a lot of money if I could work my issues out that way. Instead, the bad feelings fester like a virus. And it becomes impossible to find Patient Zero.

We also live in a punitive society. It's slowly changing but it begins in childhood. Children are punished for doing something "wrong". Schools reward "good" students and condemn "bad" ones. The justice system is based on judging what is right and wrong, good and bad. Those who violate it, whether because of lapsed judgment, poor upbringing, mental instability, or all of the above, are shunned from society, their lives changed forever, perhaps because of one mistake. So, why should we treat our selves any differently? Why on Earth would we be so loving as to let ourselves off the hook for something that happened 10 years ago?

The Healing Takes Longer Than the Damage

Why does one misstep have the ability to forge our destiny? Because we don't forgive ourselves right after it happens. Many times we don't even know it's happening— we're too young, or too traumatized, or simply not aware of the power someone's words or behavior has over us before it's too late.

Then, over time, we start to link everything together: The time your father called you lazy with the time your boss denied your raise. The way your mother called you useless with the way your wife refuses to let you get close. The damage happened quickly—one word. One glance. One simple action. But finding our way back to the source—isolating it, seeing it for what it is and then letting it go—that can take time.

Be patient with yourself. Get professional help if need be. The power of talk therapy, of bringing your damage into the light, is the first step in letting it go. There's a reason why confession has lasted so long in the Catholic religion: we have a built-in need to air our "stuff," to shine a light on those ghosts and expose them for what they are—not real.

You may not be able to see every inciting incident from your past with full clarity. That's okay. The act of forgiving ourselves is more important than the time travel. If you can't find the source for a feeling you've been carrying around your whole life, I give you full permission to let it go anyway.

Progress Not Perfection

Losing patience with ourselves doesn't serve the healing. As a matter of fact, it takes us back a few steps. Losing patience with ourselves is what got us here in the first place.

Perfection is an unattainable ideal. That's also what got us here. Again, I'm not talking about the Divine Perfection that is born in all of us. I'm speaking about an idea we have of how we're supposed to be that usually interrupts the flow of getting what we want. This idea can also keep us from moving forward, taking that leap because we're worried it won't be perfect when we try. It's a great way to keep us "safe". Please remember, perfection in this regard is never the goal. Progress is. Being able to see small increments of change or, if you're lucky, giant leaps.

EXERCISE

Getting out of our own way can sometimes be one of the hardest steps to take. This exercise, that I'm about to share with you, has helped many a client to let go of past choices and move forward to the next step.

❧

Find a photo of yourself when you were young. And not just any photo, your favorite photo, from any time when you were young.Put it on your phone or someplace where you can glance at it regularly. When you find yourself going down the path of negative talk and beating yourself up, look at that picture. Remind yourself that there was no way for your younger self to know what you know now. We tend to blame all our mistakes on our past selves, which is and isn't true. Yes, 12 year old you made a mistake, but 12 year old you did not know what you know now. Have compassion for yourself. Let yourself off the hook.

❧

Remember, compassion is the key to growth.

"Be fearless in the pursuit of what sets your soul on fire."

~ JENNIFER LEE

Gifts vs Passion

Gifts and Passions - Separately

We are half way through. Congratulations! Take a moment to celebrate that you made it this far. But now, we are about to get into the hard work. And I have a little secret for you; this was the hardest concept for me to wrap my brain around. Until I fully understood this break down, I was not able to move forward with anything. I was literally stuck in myself. It took a gut punch from life to get me to stop and see what my true gift in life was and where my passion lived. And if I'm being honest, the hardest part about this concept, especially for creatives, is that your gift and passion may have nothing to do with your talent. I'm going to say that one more time for good measure, your gifts and passion may have nothing to do with your talent. Now that we got that out of the way let's look at what exactly is a gift and a passion so you can find yours.

Webster's defines gift as a natural ability.

A gift is just that—a unique facility bestowed on us. Take a look back at your life and again, take a look at what people around you look to you for. What has been in you, something that you were just always good at without even trying? For some it may be creative, like singing or dancing. For others it might be around numbers or organizing. For me, it was helping people. I've just always been able to emotionally impact people and persuade them to see the best in themselves. The fact is, we often overlook our gift for various reasons. But when we open up to the possibilities our gifts can bring into our life, a shift will happen that allows for our WHY to become clear. Keep in mind; a gift is what we're good at doing, regardless of whether or not we find our bliss every moment we're engaged in it. In fact, sometimes our gift doesn't yield bliss at all; sometimes it simply feels like work. But—provided it doesn't pain us to do it—if we harness it, it's a way to be of use and contribute to the world.

And now for the passion. Webster's defines *passion* as an intense desire or enthusiasm for something.

Take a moment and think, is there something you would do anytime, anywhere, for free if need be. You just want to be a part; sometimes you will even pay to join. This concept goes back to Chapter 2 and finding your WHY—the idea that deep within us lies a calling to do something that brings us true joy. It causes us to completely lose track of time while we're doing it. It aligns us with our highest purpose and ultimate dream.

This is our passion.

Remember I said this was the hardest concept for me to

get? I want to share how I figured it out because it might allow you to get there for yourself. I want to start by saying that I had gotten my passion and gift all turned around. As many creatives often do, I had assumed acting was my gift. I had a talent for it and for close to a decade I made money doing it. For an actor, it doesn't get much better than that.

In fact, the only thing I felt lacking was a child of my own. Within three years I gave birth to both my beautiful daughters, Ava and Olivia. Here's where it gets real. Thankfully my daughters were both born perfectly healthy and I had an incredible village around me because life threw me a giant curveball. In what should have been the most joyous and exciting new period for me, I quickly experienced a full-on mind and body meltdown.

The days when I rushed from one audition to the next and threw a lunch into the mix were long gone. Now I could barely get out of bed. I no longer recognized myself. I had made my life bigger but had not set up a foundation to hold it. Nothing meant anything to me—not acting, not mothering, not really even life. I was terrified.

It took a dozen different doctors and months upon months of testing to tell me that I had an autoimmune disorder and it had wreaked havoc on my thyroid, throwing it completely out of whack. The news was both a blessing and a curse, but as I always say, information equals knowledge equals power, so I finally had the tools I needed to heal.

But again, getting sick and the course I needed to traverse to get well required blowing up a picture. I had to learn to love the process. You will find that this is an exercise that doesn't happen only once in a lifetime. Sometimes it will be easy and immediate and sometimes, like this particular moment in my life, it will be lengthy and painstaking and dramatic. But it's always worth it.

Here's the great irony in my own story. Giving birth, the very thing that brought me to my knees and made me feel the most inadequate, became the gateway to accessing all the power that was ahead of me. Getting to your gift and passion may not look this dramatic, it doesn't have to. I just happen to be a driven and determined person, who will not stop unless the wall hits me. It is one of my many flaws but it's also why I'm writing this book. So, I've learned to embrace the lessons, no matter how dramatic. If I hadn't been sucker punched and stopped in my tracks by two beautiful and quite frankly powerful bundles of love, I would never have been able to start painting the picture of the new me.

I have told you that I had my passion and gift all mixed up. It turned out my passion was acting, and I had been relying solely on my passion to get me through life. And as my story has illustrated, this will not keep you on your feet when life knocks you over. My main point is this: It took me a while to get my head around my idea of who I was. I had to let go of the thought that what I did defined me. Who I am does not lie in what I do for a living or even what I'm passionate about. But like so many of us, I was fixated on this idea, which only kept me imprisoned in a state of powerlessness. It wasn't until I was able to acknowledge *all* my gifts and skills that I found the key to unlock myself from the cell of my own making. I could, actually, have it all: my modern family, my acting career, and now my own business.

And here we are.

 *Finding your passion isn't just about careers and money. It's about finding your authentic self. The one you've buried beneath other people's needs.*

~ KRISTEN HANNAH

Notice I did not use the word "talent" anywhere when discussing passion. Why? Because it's not our (or anyone else's) job to link talent with passion. Having a deep-seated urge to embark on a particular path is not necessarily linked to being good at it. We *can* get good at it—become an expert even—because doing something we love for long periods of time often creates a level of mastery. But again—and let me make this point abundantly clear—we may love doing something even if we haven't won prizes in the field, or been told from birth that it's our destiny, or made oodles of money doing it.

If we love doing it, we *must* do it. It's as simple as that.

Gifts and Passion – Together

Once I allowed my gifts and passions to exist together, I was able to start creating the life I wanted, and my WHY became very clear. Now, I once again feel like I need to be honest with you. I did not come to this easily, in fact, if you talk to Melissa, I came kicking and screaming, but thank God, she was able to hold up a mirror that allowed me to see the real me.

Melissa has been a catalyst for me for the past decade. She was the one who ultimately helped refine my gifts and nurture my passions. You don't always know from where your catalyst or mirror will come. Melissa entered my life as a nanny to my two children. She was the ultimate nanny, Mary Poppins in high heels. She gave me the strength to be the best mom I could be, and be creative at the same time. She was also witness to my true calling of helping people. She watched me work with coaches and mentors, and research almost every self-empowerment strategy on the planet but I didn't have a focus. I was still trapped in my prison of "should." But Melissa is a creative at her core and because of that a business was born where more people can be reached than I could have possibly imagined. Melissa's gift for children and passion for creating new ways to tackle the everyday melded beautifully with my gifts and passions—and for that I am eternally grateful.

There are few things as tough as taking a fearless personal inventory, as they say in the 12-Step Program. It involves letting go of old ideas of who we are and gradually accepting new ones, as foreign as they may seem. This shift may cause us to feel like we're not the person we thought we were. That our embedded sense of identity was somehow wrong. That we were wrong.

My friend, Natalie, illustrates this perfectly. An actor and singer (who sang in a Heart cover band which is so uncool it's cool), Natalie was born into a billion dollar personal development company. Like most of us, she didn't realize what her gift was. She thought her ability to connect with others was better suited in the world of performing and hospitality. She resisted the family business, willing to help her parents from time to time, but wanted to keep her focus on singing, which is her passion. But then she got pregnant and was forced to run up and down the stairs of the bar she was managing. This ended up being her mirror and she realized that connecting with people was her gift, not just something she was good at and was perfectly suited for her family's business. She was finally able to see all the positives it had to offer—its flexible schedule, the fact that in many ways it was second nature to her, and she was going to be a part of continuing a family legacy, jumping into what was inherently hers. Here's what I want to drive home about Natalie's story, because of how she was raised, she was already aware of mindset and positive self-talk and all that other good stuff we've been getting into with this book. And even with that great foundation, she still had to do the work to figure out her gift and passion, and how to make it work for her. Once she was able to see clearly, she went from thinking that working in the family business would eclipse her singing to realizing that not only is it the perfect supplement to her creative work, but also that she can DO it all, HAVE it all, and BE it all.

In my parents' generation, most people had one job that they did for an entire lifetime. When they retired, they may have nurtured a golf swing or taken up pottery, but those were *hobbies*, endeavors put into a lesser category because a) they didn't necessarily pay the rent, b) they weren't mastered, and c) they were—*gasp*—fun. Things sure have changed, haven't they? According to a *Future Workplace* "Multiple Generations @ Work" Survey, 90 percent of millennials (those born between 1977 and 1997) will stay in a job less than three years. This means they could have 15 to 20 jobs over the course of their lifetimes. True, for some people a one-career life is a reality, but for most of us it's not. Reinvention and new mindsets are not only a way to keep those bills paid but they're also a way to tune into new sides of ourselves and explore them. When we think outside the box, we have the potential to create multiple revenue streams. Just think about that.

The path we're on—you (simply by having picked up this book), me, all of us—is one of constant reinvention and the shedding of old skin to make way for a new one. The more we understand that the truth of who we are is not bound to what we do, the more we can live fully in the moment. By embracing that divine perfect, we can experience the joy, pain, miracle, and even disappointment of what we're doing *right now*.

The Payoff

I have some good news for you. Being clear about our gifts versus our passion allows us to use our gifts to serve our passion. What a concept, huh? We can use what we're good at in order to do what we love!

When I mentioned how things were back in the "old days" I realize how far we've come and I encourage you to see it, too. Not that everyone in that generation did such a thing, mind you, but to wait until your golden years before we find our true bliss is a waste of a life. It's also a misinterpretation of why we've been put on this Earth in the first place. And I hope you are seeing that finding a strong WHY is key.

What does it look like to use your gifts to support your passion? Well, let's say you have a talent for numbers and are skilled at accounting. Do you know how many people break out in hives when it comes to doing their books? Why not try working as a freelance accountant/bookkeeper? You may start by charging a reasonable hourly rate and then increase it as you get more clients. You may find that having the autonomy and ownership where moneymaking is concerned frees you up to do what you really love.

Maybe you want to transition out of one field and into another. Why not try teaching what you spent a good part of your adult life doing at work? Teaching is a wonderful way to give back while also utilizing our gifts. It also affords a certain amount of autonomy so that we can focus our energies on our new project. Something to keep in mind when you are transitioning in any field, keep an eye out for a coach or mentor that is living the life that you want. Seek their guidance and allow them to be your catalyst or mirror. Let them help expose your WHY and get you on your path.

Your gifts and passions can and should be used to help you live your fullest life. And here's another thing: They don't have to have anything to do with one another. You can have a gift for crunching numbers and a passion to teach sustainable farming in a developing country. You can have a gift for languages and a passion for starting a theatre company in your hometown.

Take a breath, that was a lot. I know. Like I said, this was the hardest concept for me to get. So please don't worry if it takes you a minute or even longer to get there. When you get stuck or are unsure, try reminding yourself that your gift is that thing that you've always been doing and your passion is that thing that you always want to do.

It's not what we say out loud that really determines our lives.

It's what we whisper to ourselves that has the most power.

~ ROBERT T. KIYOSAKI

6

~~~~~~~~~~

Your Circle of Influence

O h, to be one of the lucky people born with a healthy dose of self-esteem! People who never fall into bad relationships. People who don't take years to ask for a much-deserved raise. People who believe they deserve all the blessings life has to offer and won't accept anything less. Very few of us are like this. But what if I told you that just by changing your mindset you could be one of those lucky people?

Here's what we know: Our mindset can affect everything from self-esteem to creating what we want. If we are living in a poor mindset, how do we turn it around? There are many ways and many books about flipping the mindset switch, believe me, I've read most of them. One of my favorites is Shad Helmstetter, Ph.D. In his book, *What to Say When You Talk to Yourself,* he says, "The brain simply believes what you tell it most. And what you tell it about you, it will create. It has no choice."

Enough Already

A major step towards changing your mindset is reminding ourselves—weekly, daily and hourly—that we have enough and that we *are* enough. This isn't always easy, especially if we've set goals for ourselves that we have yet to achieve. But to start from a place of "enoughness" allows us to view everything that comes after as the blessings that they are. Remember when I talked about embracing my gifts and passions? That was a mindset shift for me. I had to fully realize that there was nothing else for me to work on; I had everything I needed within me. That's not to say there isn't more to learn or fine tuning that can be applied, but I don't have to be more than me to get what I want. That's exactly what's at play when we fully grasp that we are enough right here, right now. We don't *need* as much as we thought we did. There's less grasping, less desperation. This concept is radical in a world where everywhere we turn we're being offered something that promises to make us better. But it's key to rebuilding our sense of self.

Starting a gratitude journal is a great way to enumerate what we already have and what we have accomplished. Sometimes starting a journal can be intimidating or you feel like if you can't do it every day, what's the point? I get it. Personally, I love the journal because I get to go into the store and pick the one that speaks to me, it works for me, but if it doesn't work for you, try sitting with gratitude. Take a moment each day to sit and just think about the things for which you are grateful. I have found that when we have gratitude, that "enoughness" that we talked about becomes reality.

ENOUGHNESS
The Simple Truth of Embracing You

 *Surround yourself with the dreamers
and the doers, the believers and thinkers,
but most of all, surround yourself
with those who see the greatness in you,
even when you don't see it yourself.*

~ EDMUND LEE

If life is a theatre (and I, for one, wouldn't have it any other way): Then who's in your front row? Do you have people who think you're fabulous and capable of great things? Or people who bring you down and stifle your dreams?

Life certainly *is* too short to spend with people who, whether consciously or not, dump on your dreams. A major step in the mindset shift is to take a hard look at who's in our corner. The people around us influence us in ways we're not often aware. Do you feel exhausted after having dinner with that old high school chum? There's a reason for it. She may be an energy drain and yet you feel a sense of loyalty that causes you to spend three hours a month—three hours you will never get back—listening to her woes.

Obviously when it comes to family members this can get

tricky. It's not so easy to cut your overly critical mother out of your life as much as you may wish you could. But I give you full permission to limit time spent even with family members who leave you feeling depleted. Here's the thing: As much as you try to convince yourself that you can do something to shift that dynamic, in many cases you're dealing with a person or people who are *not* doing the work you're doing, who are *not* reading the books you're reading. All the trying in the world will get you nowhere, except frustrated as hell.

The energy it takes to lift people up could be put to a thousand better uses including staying home by yourself and hanging with your cat for three hours. The energy it takes to build your sense of self-worth back up after hanging with one of your Patronizing Peeps diverts you from rocking that business meeting, or making those phone calls, or looking for friends who hold a space of infinite possibility for you.

I'm going to suggest you seek out friends who are doing *better* than you. That's right—look for them, connect with them and make them your friends, bring them into your circle of influence. Maybe you already know them, in which case call them and ask them to lunch. Maybe they're already doing what you only dream about. Maybe they have an outlook you admire. Maybe they have the discipline that you wish you had. To go back to the theater analogy, move these people into your front row. It's okay to keep people in your life that don't lift you up, they just may need to be at the box office for now.

*When you know better,
you do better.*

~ MAYA ANGELOU

Many of us feel that it's somehow "wrong" or "mean" to make a decision not to hang around a person. *They're not a bad person*, we tell ourselves. *We go way back.* I'm not suggesting that in one swift blow you cut someone from your friend roster. I'm simply saying we need to periodically reevaluate the people with whom we hang out. If whom we spend time around affects how we see ourselves, and how we see ourselves affects how we move through the world, then shouldn't we be choosy about who's taking up valuable real estate in our lives?

Your time is a huge value to you. Don't just give it away.

Self Care

I want to take a moment now to talk about health, both mental and physical. Part of having a positive mindset is self-care. I don't want to gloss over what it means to have—and ultimately tackle—deep-rooted psychological problems. If that help is needed, please do what you need to do to take care of you. Reach out and ask for help. But the intention of this book is less to delve into those issues and more to point you in a direction towards healing and a positive mindset so that is what I will focus on now.

There are ways we can start to simply take care of ourselves and make sure our mind and body are on the right track. Start noticing what you eat and drink, and how it makes you feel. Think about cutting back on the things that diminish your energy and leave you with that numbed-out feeling that foods with a high glycemic index can do. Do you exercise? You need it. Our bodies are made for moving, and we need to find a way to do that for the sake of our health and sanity as much as for an aesthetic ideal. If you don't already know it, figure out your preferred form of exercise and commit to doing it regularly. Do you like team sports or are you a solitary exerciser? Do you like to dance? Start working on developing a mindful relationship with your body. What does that mean? Set aside a relatively short amount of time— no more than an hour at a stretch—and really focus on what you're doing. Put down your phone. Don't try to catch up on your reading even on the seemingly boring treadmill or stationary bike. Try not to just "get through" it. Your body is yours for life so you may as well be on good terms with it. Find something you genuinely enjoy and a schedule to which you can commit. Set yourself up for success, not failure. You have to have a good mindset to build healthy habits. Motivation will only get you so far, if you haven't taken the time to adjust your mindset and put these habits in place, allowing time for the self-care you need will be very hard to maintain. Start slow. Put in five minutes a day that is just for you. After a week, go to 10 minutes and then 20, and eventually you will get to an hour. An hour a day, just for you. I can already hear your self-talk, trust me, you are not being selfish, you are just resetting so you can be your best self, not just for you but for those around you as well.

Faith is to believe what you do not see.
The reward of this faith
is to see what you believe.

~ ST. AUGUSTINE

Finding Faith

Okay, so we're working on our Circle of Influence, we're getting into healthy habits, and we are setting up a positive mindset. Now, we just need to have a little faith. Faith means many things to many people. To some, it means going to church every Sunday. To others, it means having a plastic Jesus figurine on the dashboard of their car. Faith is like food:

ENOUGHNESS
The Simple Truth of Embracing You

What works for some doesn't work for others. Some people love putting ketchup on everything, for others if there isn't bread, it isn't a meal. Some people love a Sunday mass; others prefer crystals and reflective meditation. It really is about what works best for you, there is no wrong way to have faith.

I'll be brief: You need to find something bigger than yourself and believe in it. That's called faith. It may not be the kind of faith that your Jewish grandmother had but it's faith nonetheless.

What does this mean, exactly? It means that we let ourselves off the hook a little bit and realize that not everything in our lives is determined by us and us alone. You know the peace that comes over you when you decide to use your GPS to find that out-of-the-way place as opposed to relying on a foggy memory of the last time you were there, three years ago?

There's a feeling of surrender even if the GPS happens to cut out. You're still behind the wheel of a two-ton vehicle so it's not like you can close your eyes. You still have to pay attention but you're just not gripping the wheel so tightly that callouses form.

Take some time to consider something bigger than yourself and commit to believing in it. Whether it's a meditation practice, or a traditional house of worship, or simply saying a prayer out loud—the miracle of faith is that, having faith in something larger than yourself enables you to have faith in yourself.

Fake It 'Til You Make It

Notice this chapter is about your best self as opposed to repairing your damaged self. Very few of us have had a perfect childhood. We all have our fair share of damage. And the truth is if we choose to look at it differently, we could say that our "damage" also makes us the unique person we are.

You can find your way back to feeling good about yourself. You can build back self-esteem. It may not happen overnight—or it may, that's possible, too—but feeling validated from a few small steps points you toward a deeper sense of confidence as you walk through the world. You may have to force your way into those steps. You may not *feel* like yourself taking them. But do them anyway.

Step into the new you even if the old you resists.

Just like that red wine stain on a white shirt, confidence oozes in and it oozes out. People notice it. Your self-esteem grows. And then one day—*poof*—you look in the mirror and see the person you've always wanted to be.

*"Do not confuse
the voice of ego with
that of intuition."*

~ ANONYMOUS

Breaking the Pattern

If you're here, I know your ego is screaming. You are working on some big changes and trust me, your ego is pushing back hard. If you started here, I suggest you read Chapters 5 and 6 first, just to get your mindset ready for the work that is to come. But what exactly is ego you may be thinking and more importantly, why is it screaming?

Ego—the word means many things to many people.

Freud defined it as the organized part of the psyche that mediates between the savage beast inside us known as the "id" and the societal influence he called the "superego." Jung described the ego as the center of consciousness, emerging separately from the sense of "wholeness" with which an individual is born. We say someone has a "big ego" when they exhibit a certain over-the-top self-confidence; and that someone has a "healthy ego" when that self-confidence seems justified.

In various spiritual traditions, the term "ego" means something else altogether. For instance, A COURSE IN MIRACLES (http://www.acim.org) describes the ego as, "... but a dream of what you really are." In some South Asian traditions, the ego is considered "maya" or "samsara," which loosely means "illusion." Deepak Chopra describes ego as, "...our self-image, not our true self. Labels, masks, images and judgments characterize it. The true self is the field of possibilities, creativity, intentions and power."

I'll stick closer to the term "ego" as it is used in a spiritual context: The part of us that considers itself separate from others, which seeks to keep us locked into an idea—wholly of our own making—of who we are and what we are meant to do. The ego is the opposite of God—or Universe—consciousness, the all-inclusive, ever-expanding force that is ours to tap into if—and when—we decide to let go of our ideas of how things are supposed to be.

Why not use another food analogy here? The ego is the lunchbox filled with the usual stuff, day in, day out: A peanut butter and jelly sandwich on white bread, an apple and a bag of chips. It may not be the most exciting choice or even your favorite choice but it's food. The opposite is an all-you-can-eat buffet with breakfast, lunch and dinner all rolled into one. Prime rib, more vegetables then you knew existed, salads with arugula, fresh tomatoes and goat cheese. But the thing is, it's behind a door. You've never actually seen the buffet. In order to get there, you would need to leave the lunchbox at home and simply trust that you'll find the buffet when it's time for lunch.

When we let go of ego, we tap into the flow of the Universe. Miracles happen. But like that buffet table behind the door, we don't know exactly what that means and how that looks. And let's be honest—that can be scary. So we lean on the ego to keep things safe and reliable.

And stuck.

Just to clarify: The ego isn't all bad. It's often the engine behind transformation because when one ego clashes with another ego, change can happen. It's also the stuff of great story. Oedipus, Scarlett O'Hara, and George Costanza were all pretty ego-driven. Abraham Lincoln, Martin Luther King Jr., and Susan B. Anthony probably all had healthy egos in order to help transform the world as they did.

Ego as a Ninja

But make no mistake: As much as the ego can inspire change, its main goal, its primary function if you will, is to keep us locked in a certain way of being that *feels* good but may not ultimately serve us. If we don't stop our ego from running the show, we'll never get to the next level in life. But here's what's tricky: We don't know when this is happening. When the ego speaks, it speaks in code. It's like the secret agent that we think is a family man working in insurance but in reality is helping topple foreign governments. It's covert, stealthy, and sends messages you think are helpful but will ultimately kill your dreams and squelch your spirit.

Here are some seemingly innocuous messages the ego sends us:

I don't feel like it.

I'm not qualified.

I'm not prepared.

I may not have a good experience.

My family doesn't do things like that.

I don't do things like that.

It's probably best if I sit this one out.

I don't have time.

It doesn't fit my schedule.

I didn't get the job because the people are stupid.

I don't work for less than [fill in the blank].

I don't date people who [fill in the blank].

I don't want to get hurt.

The ego loves to complicate things. It gives lengthy explanations as to why something is impossible and why you should avoid doing it. Or, as with the phrases above, it makes up rules just for the sake of rules. It loves drama, gossip, and intrigue. It casts you as an innocent victim or an uninvolved bystander. *I can't believe this keeps happening to me,* it exclaims, like the damsel in distress it pretends to be. Really? It knows full well what it's doing, make no mistake. *I was just minding my own business when she started to yell at me out of the blue.* It's a piranha feeding off insecurity and denial, and abdicates you from personal responsibility. It concocts a thesis, which by all accounts is brilliant, but in the end, who cares? You're still stuck in the muck.

As you can see, I get pretty worked up talking about the ego. Maybe because I'm no stranger to its covert ops. As a matter of fact, when writing this book, my ego and I went mano-a-mano. I'd written two chapters, then set them aside. Then, a few days later, I read them again and hit the roof. *I can't do this*, I screamed (in my head). *Who am I to put my life on display like this and my thoughts in full view? Stop the book*, I thought, *I want to get off!*

Shame got involved and if I had given into it, real damage could've been done. So what did I do? Obviously, you're reading the book now, right? I did nothing. Or rather, I stopped and chose again. I didn't work from a place of reaction. I sat with my feelings and eventually realized it was my ego rearing its ugly head. I also consulted my "experts"— people like my business partner, Melissa, who is the exact person you want when your ego threatens to firebomb your life. She talked me out of my craziness and put everything in perspective. Eventually I calmed down. That's the thing: Unless you're an enlightened master, you have an ego that always needs to be checked. For better or worse, it's here to stay. But if we learn to recognize it, and even work with it, we can become the forward-moving people we're meant to be, and have the life we're meant to have.

Don't you dare underestimate the power of your own instinct.

~ BARBARA CORCORAN

You may be wondering, *if I can't rely on my ego to prevent me from getting hurt, how will I avoid a potentially dangerous situation?* Excellent question.

That's where our instincts come in.

Instincts are built-in mechanisms to keep the species alive. In his book, *The Gift of Fear*, Gavin de Becker (http://gavindebecker.com) discusses how women—and men—manage to avoid threats to their life, simply by paying attention to that little voice inside their head that told them something was "not right". In the moment, we may not even be aware of the stimuli we're picking up, but when we stay present and listen to that voice, we keep ourselves safe.

And when I say "safe" in this context, I mean, we stay alive. There's a difference between safe as our ego would have us be and the safe our basic instincts were put in place to ensure. It's important to know the difference. When the ego wants to keep you "safe" it may be tricking you into thinking it's keeping you out of harm's way, but it's really just trying to keep you in the status quo and, frankly, slightly miserable. I'm not saying that we should all be jumping out of planes; I'm referring to the things in life we secretly want but require a leap of faith and a break from the routine.

Tell-Tale Signs

How can you tell the difference between ego and instinct? It's not easy because, again, the ego is a tricky creature. But a big guideline for knowing if your ego is speaking and pretending to be your instinct is response versus reaction. Your instincts respond; your ego reacts. I'm just going to say that one more time for good measure—your instincts respond; your ego reacts.

What does this mean exactly? A response is an appropriate answer to either a question or a suggestion. Scratch that—it may be completely inappropriate but if it comes from an authentic place, that's fine too. A reaction is an emotional lashing-out that usually means the ego felt threatened and smacked the person doing the threatening upside the head. Or rather you, governed by this force, did the smacking. My reaction to seeing my life on paper was just that: A reaction, not a response. I didn't smack a person so much as I smacked my dreams down. And—this is another gauge—I didn't realize it until later.

How do you respond when a friend or loved one makes a suggestion? Do you immediately put up a defense, or do you hear them out, even if it was unsolicited and you don't necessarily agree with it?

What about when you don't get a job? Do you react by attacking the job or yourself for "failing" to get it? Say you had a gut reaction regarding your potential boss. He made a few inappropriate comments. If you were using your instinct, you would be thinking, *Nope, not for me.* An ego response wants the job anyway. Why? Because the ego constantly seeks validation. The ego needs to get the job to feel worthy.

What about in the dating realm? You meet someone you feel in your gut isn't right for you. He or she spoke harshly about an ex, which shed light onto their own set of baggage. Do you try to win him or her simply to prove you can? In terms of relationships, do you stay in them because you need to feel wanted even if they've run their course?

These are important guidelines for being able to discern between two very powerful forces within ourselves, ego and instinct. Start paying attention to whether you react or respond—how and to what. Just as awareness is the first step towards change, noticing your ego at work is the first step in keeping it in check.

 More the knowledge lesser the ego,
lesser the knowledge more the ego...

ENOUGHNESS
The Simple Truth of Embracing You

~ ALBERT EINSTEIN

One of the ways we clarify if our ego or our instinct is at work is by saying "yes." *Do you want to come to my party?* Yes. *I have a cool job you might be right for. Interested?* Yes. *Would you help me with some work I have? I'll pay you.* Yes. *Want to help me set up an illegal business? I'll give you a percentage from all the money I know I'm going to make off of it.* Um, no.

This isn't an exercise in keeping yourself mindlessly busy. This is a way to start getting out of your own way and recognizing when you might have said "no" to things simply because they didn't fit with your "plan". Start saying "yes" to things you may have said "no" to before. Count how many yeses you collect. Remember: You have the right to decide "no" later. But for now, say "yes". And a funny thing happens when you start to do this: you get more in tune with your instincts so that things that really don't sit well with you scream it, loud and clear.

Notice how this makes you feel. Do your hands get

clammy? Is your heart beating faster? Do you feel weirdly vulnerable? Excellent! That means you're uncomfortable. You're uncomfortable because you're breaking a pattern. You're actually rewiring your brain. Saying "yes" starts to remove those fears, one level of discomfort at a time creating a new mindset.

Positive thinking takes us most of the way. There is a reason why affirmations, intentions, and law of attraction works, it's not magic. The brain is the most powerful computer we have, it will search out whatever we tell it, positive or negative. This is why we have to be so diligent about what we feed it. Our body and mind want to feel good. But please don't confuse comfort with feeling good, these can be two very different things. Often feeling comfortable keeps us in the same place. Feeling comfortable is actually *bad* for us in the long run. You see, no one has found their dream in the comfort zone.

Your dream has to be bigger than your fears because guess what—if your fear wasn't in your way, your dreams would be happening.

Taking time to understand our patterns, seeing where we react versus respond, putting in the "yes" to start the rewiring process, all these things help us get our ego out of our way. In doing this work myself, I have found this rule to be vital to keep my own ego in check, action cures fear.

When in doubt, set a goal, reveal an intention and boldly take an action.

"Success is not final, failure is not fatal; it is the courage to continue that counts."

~ WINSTON CHURCHILL

*The secret to having
it all is knowing
you already do.*

~ ANONYMOUS

8

The Soundboard

I'm always amazed at the metaphors we throw out when we describe our lives. We say we have "a lot of balls in the air" when we're talking about being busy. We're "taking the bull by the horns" when we're feeling powerful and in control; and we're "spinning plates" when we have a million things of varying stripes going on at once. We say these things with pride. If there were a gold medal awarded for spinning the most plates for the longest amount of time, we want it.

Let's think about this for a moment.

Balls in the air? Plates spinning over our heads? Both of these sound extremely stressful to me, and I'm just sitting at my desk with a cup of coffee. Isn't everyone afraid of fumbling the balls and crashing the plates? I sure am. Is gravity really that reliable? My over 40 body will tell you it is not. And then there's the idea of taking a charging bull by the horns. *By the horns?* If you choose to take a bull by its horns, you may want to rethink your commitment to the earthly realm. No—when you really consider them, these sayings stir up a feeling of chaos. That is exactly what we *don't* want in our lives. These images call to mind a precarious state of being in which, at any moment, one aspect of our lives can get completely out of balance and pull everything down with it.

It's just a saying, you're thinking. Of course we're not grabbing the horns of an actual bull. But here's the thing: Images and ideas have immense power over us. Theories abound, from the scientific to the metaphysical, on the subject of how our thoughts create our reality. A subtle message we send ourselves can tip us into a stressful state, even if we're not actually *doing* anything particularly stressful. We're just using a stressful image as an organizing principle.

I have a better way. Are you ready?

Have you ever been to a concert and turned away from the shrieking crowd to see the guy sitting behind that ridiculous amount of equipment, who looks like he's just come back from a year-long meditation retreat, or eaten a pound of magic mushrooms, or both? He—and I say "he" because most often it is a he—is the most relaxed person in the room. He's so chill you can't stop staring at him even if you have absolutely no idea what he's doing. You just sense that if he gets up to use the bathroom, the entire show might fall apart.

That, my friends, is the sound guy. That monster piece of equipment he's sitting in front of is a soundboard.

What does he do? Why does he get to be the great and wonderful Oz? I know this much: A sound guy constantly adjusts levels. He "mixes" music so that what we ultimately hear is a perfect blend of components at any given moment. The result is a seamless piece of music, as opposed to a horn section that blows the keyboards away or a buzzing amp that drowns out the backup vocals. When he amplifies one instrument, he lowers another. But he doesn't yank the button up from low to high in one split second so our eardrums are blown to bits. He moves one button up while he moves the other down—*gradually*. And he's paying close attention to how things sound while he's doing it. He's—yes—tuned in. Constantly. He's Buddha and Bill Gates rolled into one.

Why am I telling you this, you ask? We're not at a concert and some of us can't carry a tune to save our lives.

Because instead of seeing your life as your grandmother's china being hurled into the air, I want you to see your life as a soundboard. I want you to imagine yourself as that cool-as-a-cucumber sound person who intuitively knows how to adjust the levels of life without breaking a sweat.

What It Looks Like

It looks like doing a little bit of everything every day. Moving the "levels" that make up the components of your life forward a little bit at a time. And being "tuned in" enough to know when to pull some things back. It means mixing what you love to do with what you need to do in one big, harmonious opera that is your life. It means being patient with yourself if you don't see instant results. Instant results may cause an eardrum to blow, remember? It means trusting that your efforts, however minor they may feel, will lead to a dramatic shift in the way you live your life.

Thinking of your life as a soundboard allows you to delegate energy, time and focus. It puts you squarely in the driver's seat of your life as you make definitive choices in terms of how much effort you want to put toward something. But—here's the best part—it takes away the stress that comes with being afraid you'll drop your spinning plates if you need to adjust the radio. Spinning plates gives the impression that everything in life takes the same energy. The soundboard lets us play with levels, tones and nuances.

I'm Making a List and Checking It Twice (or Six Times)

You know those lists you love to make? The ones that start off on a crisp sheet of paper and by the end of the week are dog-eared and scribbled on? The ones that catapult you out of bed in the middle of the night just so you can add something before you forget it forever? I'm a bit of a list-maker myself, but I'm not entirely convinced that my lists actually make me as productive as I'd like to think they do. Here's the thing: A list creates a sense of hierarchy. The item at the top is the most pressing, with the level of importance dwindling as the list progresses. Sometimes seeing our lives this way is important—if we're focusing on a specific goal like leaving town or planning a wedding. But life is made up of many elements of varying tones and shades. It's a dynamic web of interconnected components.

Is work more important than health? Ask someone who's been suffering from illness and then tell me it is. And what is "health" anyway? In the end, it can mean everything from seeing friends, to traveling the world, to taking vitamins.

Seeing your life as a soundboard that includes *every* aspect, to be toned down or up as needed, gives every facet value.

If you think about it, lists tend to be more about what we *should* do and less about what we *get to* do. Isn't that why we make them in the first place? So we can feel productive and accomplished just for having written a line item on a piece of paper regardless of whether we actually *do* it? Ever wonder why that line item keeps appearing on every new list we make? As if the simple act of writing the new list will somehow assuage the guilt we feel over not having completed the task. Do you see where I'm going with this? Do you see the dysfunction?

Stop *shoulding* on yourself. Stop it now.

We're all guilty of it. I've had "clean out the garage" on my list for six years now. But too many of us either live for what we *should* be doing and/or suffer the guilt over *not* doing it. This is the opposite of having a big life, my friends.

Thinking of life in terms of a soundboard gets us to focus on what we *want* to do. Take my friend, Theresa, who is a real estate developer and decided to train for a marathon. She didn't need to spend every weekend running 10 plus miles under the broiling Southern California sun. It didn't necessarily advance her career or make her more money. It certainly didn't do her laundry or get her car washed. She did it because she *wanted to*. She did it to prove she could, with the added bonus of getting in great shape and meeting new people (who were also presumably getting into great shape and looking to meet new people).

Changing our outlook in terms of what we spend our time doing lets us enjoy it more. Thinking of a task as less of a "should" and more of a "get to" puts us in touch with the things that make us happy. It helps us build, brick by brick, the life we want.

 *Respond to any call that makes your soul happy.*

~ RUMI

I want you to have a big life. I want you to have the career you want and the relationships that nurture you. I want you to be healthy physically and mentally, to feel true joy when you spend time with your kids, go for drinks with your girlfriends and fire up the grill with the neighbors. I want you to be able to do what you love well into your golden years without aches and pains—or worse, serious illness—cramping your style.

I also want you to give yourself permission to have a full life and know it can only support you in your desire to own your own business or become a great musician. Ignoring things that don't directly relate to the immediate needs of career and family will ultimately affect career and family negatively if we don't tend to them.

Let's look at how one affects the other. Ever notice what happens when you spend too much time at work? You suddenly realize you need a night out and you need it badly. It creeps up slowly and then goes off like a car alarm. Sure—intense focus for a concentrated amount of time can sometimes be absolutely necessary: You're meeting a deadline or you're short-staffed at work. But when one aspect of your life outweighs all the others—when the vocals are wailing way above the drums—things get a little screwy.

Equalizing and Harmonizing

What if we began to change our idea of what it means to be a successful person? We'll focus on this in the next chapter, but what if we took away some of the things we can't control—oodles of money coming at us, world renown— and replaced it with something we can? What if we saw our lives as one integrated whole, no different from an ocean or a forest, where one form of life affects another in a very real way?

There's a lot of talk these days about balance. Everyone wants it; no one seems to have it. I'm going to come clean and say I don't like the word myself, and I rarely use it.

The words I use fall right in line with the soundboard image: I want you to think of your life as being *equalized* and *harmonized.*

What's the difference? Like the spinning plates image, balance can create a sense of stress. With the idea of balance is also the fear that one day something will cause life to fall *out of balance.* One day something will tip the scales and pull everything down with it.

Equalizing and harmonizing are an ongoing process. Trees don't stop growing in a forest. And if one dies, the process of decay jumps in and takes over. A healthy river doesn't stop flowing. Like the sound guy, we never stop adjusting those levels, pulling one back while moving the other forward. For months, Theresa was focused on that Sunday when she'd be running 26.2 miles through the streets of Los Angeles. It wasn't that she was any *less* busy at work. She didn't stop feeding herself or seeing her friends. She just dialed some areas of her life back to focus on a goal that was a lifelong dream. Because she knew that once it was reached she could dial those other areas back up.

Your job. Your career (if it's separate from your job).

Your health and well-being. Your family. Your friends. Your charities and/or volunteer activities. Your hobbies. Your "me" time. These, and then some, are all levels on the soundboard that is your life. Sometimes external circumstances require us to move one aspect forward, sometimes we just want to give something our focus for a while. But here's what's important: We have to give ourselves permission to pull back on certain things and trust that they'll be there when we come back for them. Lowering the level of the drums doesn't mean the drumbeat disappears. It doesn't mean the drummer walks offstage and goes to lunch. He's still doing his job and that job is contributing to the overall sound.

And one more thing: You *can* go to lunch. Unlike spinning plates, which requires constant attention and movement, you can leave the soundboard and take a bathroom break. How does this translate in real-world terms? Say you get sick and need to take time off. Say you get the opportunity of a lifetime to take a cruise to Alaska. You may have to adjust levels a bit when you come back but it's not a complete reboot. Your life won't come to a dead stop.

That super Zen sound person is you. You are the master of your life and all it encompasses. The soundboard. It's all about focusing your energy and getting rid of stress and "should".

The great thing about the soundboard, and what I truly love about it is, you can start at any time. You can wake up tomorrow and have this new way of thinking in place. Start by taking a moment, make a list of what you have going on in your life. What is getting the most attention? What is getting the least attention? What is missing? From there, start to plan your day, your week, your month. And before you know it, you will be able to handle what life hands you without fritzing out.

"Acknowledging the good that you already have in your life is the foundation for all abundance."

~ ECKHART TOLLE

9

Accepting
Your Success

We live in a world that, for the most part, defines success very narrowly. When I say "we" I don't mean to assume that the only people reading this book live in the Western Hemisphere, or that as individuals apart from the collective we don't have our own ideas about what it means to be successful. But the notion of success, one that began to flourish in America around the mid-to-late nineteenth century and has managed to spread to other parts of the world, has a very specific association. When we talk about success as a general concept, we tend to talk about it in relation to money.

You see the new Porsche parked in your neighbor's driveway. You see the new pool being dug. Your brain automatically associates those material goods with the concept of success. You may even say to yourself, "Wow. Ms. Jones has really achieved a level of success in her life." What if Ms. Jones hates her job so much she throws up before going to work every day? What if she's in debt up her to her eyeballs and therefore can't quit said hated job? Do the Porsche and the pool negate these intangible factors that color this person's life?

Don't get me wrong: I do not wish misery on Ms. Jones, or anyone, and I would discourage even a healthy dose of *schadenfreude*—and just in case you need to brush up on your German, this is when you get pleasure in someone else's misfortune. I'm also open to the idea that Ms. Jones may have a Porsche, a pool, a job she delights in, and a storybook marriage. Ms. Jones may be so happy she sings arias in the shower every morning.

But this is not about Ms. Jones. This is about you (although we'll circle back to her later).

Do you feel successful? It doesn't matter whether anyone else does. Conversely, do you feel lacking because your life isn't filled with certain accepted trappings of success? I'm not sure who was the first to say it but one of my favorite quotes of all time applies to this very thing:

What other people think of you is none of your business.

Blowing Up the Picture (Again)

For years my friend, Jeanette, measured herself against her more "successful" friends. Notice how I put quotes around that word. She came to Los Angeles to write for the screen with a group of friends who had also come to Los Angeles to write for the screen. But within a few years, they were writing for network television shows and she was still churning out scripts that took up valuable real estate in a drawer. She was still working as an assistant while they *had* assistants. She'd go to dinner parties at her friends' homes in the Hollywood Hills (with pools, of course) and before someone could even hand her a cocktail, her mood would plummet and she'd start to feel horrible. She'd compare their spacious digs with her tiny apartment. She wouldn't even try to discuss her own work because she automatically felt it was inferior to theirs, simply because it hadn't brought in the same kind of money. By the time she'd leave these parties, she'd worked herself into such a state of self-loathing that it would take days for her to reemerge. She was stuck in the game of comparing. She couldn't see what she had actually accomplished, all that she saw was that her writing wasn't making her oodles of money.

Jeanette and I hadn't met each other yet, but had I known her then, I would have pointed out the things she *had* accomplished: Writing plays, one of which she self-produced, cultivating a tight community in a city not necessarily known for tight communities and gaining valuable skills in administrative positions. Lucky for Jeanette, and for me, because I love watching people step into the life they've always wanted, we did meet right when she made a major shift in what she was working on. She had taken the bold step of joining my weekly women's group. She was able to now see her accomplishments right in front of her. Her entire sense of herself and her creative potential shifted. She found her "voice".

Before, she was stuck in the comparing game, but this time I was there to help her see her success. She was able to now see that she had the luxury of finding her voice because she didn't have a demanding career. She didn't have to write for someone else's show and therefore adopt their voice. She could cultivate her own. *Not* having what her friends had made this possible. It bought her time and space to explore sides of herself that most likely she wouldn't have explored had she been granted entry into a high-paying and high-stress career track. Even though she doesn't own a home with a pool—*yet*—or drive a fancy car—*yet*, Jeanette is able to see that she is successful. At the end of the day she has changed how she measures her success, it is no longer linked to her bank account.

Do you have a garden you tend to devotedly? Do you feel an immense sense of accomplishment for being able to pay your kid's college tuition? Do you have a group of friends you cook for, and listen to and bolster, and who do the same for you? Any one of these things constitutes success. Success, as I said in the last chapter, is when all aspects of your life are working together in harmony. Success is allowing joy into as many aspects of our world as possible. Success *can* be about money—I'm by no means downplaying the importance, comfort and satisfaction of having money—but money does not define success.

YOU define success.

You define success when you stop looking at what you don't have and focus on what you do have. You define it when you celebrate your triumphs, big and small. You define it when you participate fully in *all* aspects of your life.

You've been put on this planet to do something. What it is and how you go about it varies from one person to the next. Besides, if *you* can't recognize your achievements, how do you expect other people to see them?

How do I define success?
Let me tell you, money's pretty nice.
But having a lot of money does not
automatically make you a successful person.
What you want is money and meaning.
You want your work to be meaningful,
because meaning is what brings the real
richness to your life.

~ OPRAH WINFREY

My Own Mother

My mother illustrates this perfectly. My parents have been married for over 50 years. They raised me and now they're an integral part of my children's lives. Because my father has always been the breadwinner (and they're of another generation), my mother didn't "have to work". But for the past 10 years, she's taught yoga to seniors. She gets paid, but it's a small amount, more of a token for services rendered. But that's okay—she doesn't do it for the money. She does it because she loves teaching yoga and she loves the people who take her class and, ultimately, she loves being of service in this way.

Raised a child. Being an essential part of her granddaughters' lives. Being married for over 50 years. Bringing yoga to a community that may not have had the opportunity to experience it otherwise. She's not running a multinational corporation or getting a million hits on her YouTube channel but who's to say she's not living a successful life?

Conversely, before my girls were born, there was a period of time when my acting career was soaring. I'd been on a soap opera. I had commercials running. From the outside it looked like the success was just rolling in. And yet, I've never felt so unsuccessful in my life.

Why? Because despite what I just itemized, it didn't feel like enough. I simply didn't see how lucky I was. I only saw what I *didn't* have—the shows I *wasn't* on and the career I didn't have. I was allowing other people to define my success for me. If I could go back and talk to my then self, I would have listed my achievements in capital letters on a white board and, frankly, I would have been pissed off at myself if I still didn't get it. It was only much later, when I'd experienced a bona fide dry spell, that I realized how successful I'd been. That's why I'm committed to helping others recognize the success in their lives, even if they themselves don't.

We do it to ourselves. We do it by not moving past our ideas of how things *should* be. We do it with the benchmarks we set and the hurdles we create. We set ourselves up for failure as a way of keeping ourselves safe (there's that ego again). We do it to keep from soaring way beyond our wildest imagination. We do it to prove we were never worthy in the first place.

Ever notice how some people celebrate their wins, however—and I use quotes here—as "small" as they might be? And sometimes you find yourself thinking, *gee—that's not such a big deal. What's he/she getting so excited about?* What they are getting excited about, what they are celebrating, is that they set a goal, however small, and achieved it. If you want, we can look back at my story. The reason I wasn't able to see the success in the moment is because I hadn't set goals, I hadn't found my WHY, I was just letting life happen to me. I can tell you, without any doubt in my mind, the success I have now is fully celebrated and realized. I now have goals and when I reach them, I ring that bell. It doesn't matter if it took me a day or three years to achieve. It all matters.

Our wins are ours for the celebrating because no one knows what we went through to get to them better than we do. It's not arrogant and self-serving; in fact, quite the opposite. It's arrogant *not* to appreciate the gains we've made when we make them. Acknowledging our achievements sends a direct message of gratitude not only to ourselves but to the forces in the Universe that helped us get there.

 Comparison is the thief of joy.

~ THEODORE ROOSEVELT

When You Compare You Always Lose

One of the reasons we fail to see ourselves as successful is because we do what Jeanette did: We compare ourselves to the Ms. Joneses of the world. Oftentimes, we see in others what we could never see in ourselves. Or we compare someone who's in the middle of their career to ourselves right when we're starting out. Our mind doesn't make the distinction; it simply sets our psyche off on a downward journey that ends in a pool of tears, booze, or both.

Leave Ms. Jones out of it. Don't compare your insides to other peoples' outsides.

Only YOU can live your truth.

Don't get me wrong—a healthy dose of envy isn't all bad. It's human nature and to deny it can cause us to beat up on ourselves. If we can take notice of it without letting that green slime pollute our insides, we can use it to remind ourselves of what we really want. Remember: It's not a zero-sum game. If your friend's online business is flourishing, it doesn't mean yours can't also. If you feel a twinge of envy or jealousy when you hear about your friend getting her nonprofit off the ground, there may be a budding altruist in you, too.

I get that you want more but consider this: Don't confuse that desire with the idea of not having enough. Don't live in the lack, live in the abundance. And guess what? As always, the antidote for feeling like you don't have enough is: Gratitude

For Gratitude's Sake

Make a list of what you're grateful for. Do it every day. Watch how your idea of what you have changes.

When we stop living in lack, when we start setting goals and achieving them, when we're clear about our WHY, we start to measure our success with our actual happiness. And don't be surprised if that doesn't start to make a difference in your bank account.

"It's not too late to fall in love with your life."

~ WAYLON H. LEWIS

It's not going to be easy.
But it's worth it.

~ ALISON ROBERTSON AND
A MILLION OTHER PEOPLE

10

Stop & Start Again

Congratulations—you made it. You're almost at the end of this book. And whether that means you started at page one and read every word and did every exercise, or you skipped around, you've devoted time and energy to making a positive change in your life. You've opened yourself up to the possibility of transformation. And guess what? That simple opening means that transformation will occur.

Good News and Bad News

Now I have some good news and some bad news. Let's start with the bad news. It may not always be easy. As a matter of fact, I can pretty much guarantee it won't be easy every step of the way. You'll have days when you won't even recognize the new person whose body you're inhabiting. You'll be amazed at how your outlook has changed—how certain things don't get to you the way they used to, or how you're saying "yes" to life like you never did before. Then you'll have days when you feel like you're backsliding into the same issues that dogged you long before you picked up this book. You'll use words like "always" (as in, "Why is it *always* like this?"), and "never" (as in, "Things *never* work out for me"). Then you'll ride it out and get yourself back on track.

And trust me. You will get back on track. That's the good news.

The other good news is: it's worth it.

This is the life you always wanted, remember? The one you admired in other people and wondered why it was beyond your grasp. Well, I'm here to tell you it's not. You're already living it as we speak.

Knocked off Track

Often people will be around friends and family who can't quite see the person we are becoming. I have to hold myself back from shouting, "No! Don't go!" One, it's not really my business whom you decide to spend time with. Two, you're reading a book, if you hear my voice shouting at you, we may have a bigger problem than your friends and family jumping on board your new self train.

Family of origin, friends we've known forever, even our own children (if they're grown) can bring out the worst (and the best) in us. For this purpose, I'll focus on the worst. This particular group of people can send us right back to feeling— and acting—like the troubled person we once were. Friends and family don't always recognize the changes that we've made. Our parents may still see us as dependent children. Our friends may still want us to fit in the box we were in when we met. Our children may still not see us as full human beings. This can cause intense frustration, especially when we're in the midst of a radical transformation. We plead, *why can't they see me for who I really am?* The answer lies in a multitude of reasons, none of them as important as you remaining committed to your purpose, regardless of the doubters. But also remember, it's taken you a moment to get here. It's okay to give your friends and family a chance to catch up.

One way to stay focused is to set up a support system that reminds us of who we really are. Because let's face it: You are no longer the person you were even five minutes ago. We humans are gifted with the ability to constantly reinvent ourselves and (as I've said before) I give you full permission to limit the time you spend with people who can't or won't see you in the fullest flower of your potential. This, tricky though it may be, includes family.

Have a friend (or six), a therapist and/or a coach on hand before, during and after a trip back home. If things get tense, excuse yourself from the Thanksgiving meal to telephone someone who can act as a mirror for the person you truly are, and the one you're coming into. Agree on a code word—SOS is my favorite—that you can text and arrange for a phone conversation.

You may feel guilty for becoming more than your people expected you to be. You may feel like you're leaving family and friends behind or worse—simply not getting along with the folks who once were close. They may see things differently or aren't on board with the new you or both.

It's an uncomfortable feeling and you'll feel the urge to "fix" things rather than experience it. Often that may have been your role—to be the peacemaker. Sound at all familiar? It won't be easy but I urge you to try as hard as you can, not to backslide into this pattern, but rather understand that a family and close groups of friends are made up of complex dynamics. When one person changes it places a mirror on the others, making them see their own entrenched patterns. They may not like this. But that, my friend, is not your problem to solve.

Try, if you can, to sit with the feelings as opposed to acting on them. Which brings me to my next point…

Sit with It

Friends and family aren't always the culprit for sending us into a downward spiral. Most of the time we bring it on ourselves. Old feelings of hurt and rejection can resurface and bring up feelings we thought we'd long worked through.

The first step is to head the negative thinking off at the pass. As I've discussed, when feelings of guilt, shame, and blame get involved, it becomes much more difficult to isolate the original feeling and identify it.

Try sitting with an emotion—in this case I'm talking about a negative one—and simply allow yourself to feel it. As humanist and psychologist, Carl Rogers (http://www.simplypsychology.org/carl-rogers.html) wrote, "The curious paradox is, when I accept myself just as I am, then I can change." Tara Brach (https://www.tarabrach.com), in her book, *Radical Acceptance,* discusses the value of being aware of what's going on inside us with focus that's clear and nonjudgmental. The idea is to witness it as if it were a separate entity with a life all its own. *It's interesting. I'm feeling some shame over my book proposal being rejected and that surprises me. I really thought I had moved on from that feeling.* You'd be surprised how quickly it passes when you fully give yourself over to it. This is because we're wired to do almost anything to avoid pain. And it's in the avoidance that the pain develops what can almost be thought of as "secondary illnesses"—byproducts that can become more problematic than the original feeling itself. They leave the initial pain untreated and cause it to fester.

If you're going through hell,
keep going.

~ WINSTON CHURCHILL

As initially uncomfortable as it may be, being present with our feelings allows us to be fully alive. By sitting with a feeling and letting it wash over us, we let go of labeling things "good" and "bad". All of a sudden, things just are.

You'll become very mindful of how other people deal with feelings the minute you become more tuned into them. You'll notice how your friends and family respond to your bearing witness in this way. Do they allow you to have your feelings by simply listening? Do they try to "fix" you? Or worse, do they urge you to deny that the feeling even exists?

Take a note of this. You don't have to tell your sister that after all these years you realize she's a big-time control freak. You don't have to call out Aunt Ida on her need to be doing something every waking minute of the day. Simply notice it. And maybe glance up at the heavens and whisper a very quiet, "Thank you," for having the guts and support to become the shining star that you are and always were.

"You are braver then you believe, stronger then you seem, and smarter than you think."

~A.A. MILNE

That Old Story

As you begin to notice feelings in a more detached way, try to be mindful of something being an "old story". My friend, Barb, used to get stressed about deadlines. She'd work herself into a lather before a proposal was due or a trip was to happen, and then spend the following days or weeks recovering from the stress of it all. This was not the healthiest way to live.

After a few meetings together, she began to realize that never in her life had she not gotten done what needed to be done. She'd never missed a deadline or a plane, so why stress about it? Her stress around deadlines was an old story that didn't serve her anymore.

In Barb's case, the story wasn't based on fact. Other times, we believe something to be true based on an experience from our past that we've long moved past. We remember being told we were lazy and therefore overcompensate to prove we're not. But what if we realize that we were never lazy when it really counted? What if our concept of ourselves as lazy is simply an old story that demands revision? As we start to transform, it's important to recognize an old story when you see—or feel—one, and remind yourself that's not who you are anymore.

The sooner that we can manage to separate ourselves from old stories, the sooner we can move on from old ways of thinking. Holding onto an old story keeps us fastened to an idea about who we are that no longer serves us.

When you catch yourself acting on the basis of an old story: STOP AND CHOOSE AGAIN. You are not trapped in the old ways. You have the power to pause and go in another direction.

Shortening Recovery Times

As we become more in tune, we get better at recovering more speedily from events that may have caused us to be laid up for untold lengths in the past. This is a good thing. Make sure you understand that I'm not suggesting you ignore a feeling and just "get over it." I'm simply giving you permission to move through a negative experience faster.

You have things to do. You have a magic wand to wave, remember?

It Doesn't Stop Here

Growth never stops.

Evolution is ongoing.

A commitment to transformation is lifelong.

Be Bigger.

You got this.

You're not altering the truth about yourself; you're getting more in touch with what you want.

This book will always be here if you need it. Come back, read a few lines or the whole thing over again. Remember that you—yes, you—are absolutely perfect the way you are. Your growth and change simply magnify that perfection.

And I'm so proud of you for embarking on the journey.

*"I don't want you to lose what
you want because you don't know how to
handle your worth.
Allowing yourself to be who you
are = "Enoughness."*

~ALISON ROBERTSON

CPSIA information can be obtained
at www.ICGtesting.com
Printed in the USA
LVHW030730150719
624095LV00001B/186/P

9 780578 471457